Th[illegible]
Awakening

When will the Church fervently pray for it?

Terry D. Slachter

Published by

Published by
Project Philip Publishing
4180 44th SE
Grand Rapids, MI 49512
www.projectphilipministries.org

ISBN: 978-0-9884202-4-3

First Printing, 2014

Design by Angel J. Grit

Dedicated to my grandson Kaleb with the hope and prayer that he and his entire generation will experience a true spiritual awakening.

And with gratitude to my mother Susan (Wilcox) Slachter who is now home with her Lord celebrating.

Dr. Terry D. Slachter is the Executive Director of Project Philip Ministries and Project Philip Publishing. He has served in the parish ministry for over twenty years where he taught, and led by example, the need for fervent prayer. And now, as executive director of Project Philip, he is both encouraging and equipping churches and individual Christians to sow the seed of the gospel in every household in America with fervent prayer.

Project Philip Publishing

Table of Contents

A Great Awakening in the 21st century?

When will the church begin to fervently pray for it?

Answer: When the Church becomes disgusted

Answer: When the Church becomes passionately concerned for the next generation

Answer: When the Church becomes convicted of God's displeasure

Answer: When the Church becomes submissive to Christ

Answer: When the Church becomes aware of God's Promises

Answer: When the Church becomes Jealous

A Great Awakening in the 21st Century?

These are the words of him who holds the seven stars.
I know your deeds; you have a reputation of being alive,
but you are dead. Wake up! (Rev. 3:1-2)

Awakening . . . what is it?

The term "awakening" has often been used to describe a supernatural, divine influence, which restores the joy of God's salvation to apathetic Christians; awakens the spiritually dead in the Church to their spiritual and moral condition; and leads many people from outside of the Church to the Christian Faith. There have been times throughout Church history when the awakening of the Church was considered "great," because it was not limited to a certain church or region, but was instead general, often covering many regions, denominations and countries. Great awakenings have also shaped cultures and geo-political landscapes in dramatic ways that lasted for generations.

It has been my pleasure to study these great Spirit-led movements in the Church over the past twenty years, particularly the ones in the eighteenth and nineteenth centuries. From all of my reading and historical research, I believe that every great awakening the Lord has brought about in His Church has developed progressively in five stages. The Second Great Awakening, the focus of this book, best illustrates these five stages.

Stage One: Culturally-accepted Immorality and Spiritual Indifference

Amid times of natural disaster or even financial or political unrest, God is working behind the scenes, preparing hearts to hear the gospel message. He challenges the man-made idols and philosophies of the day in much the same way Elijah challenged the prophets of Baal on Mt. Carmel when Israel was suffering under famine and drought. Fearful times challenge and discredit our man-made messiahs.

As the world tries to fashion newer idols and seeks other messiahs to help them in their time of trouble, the increase of idolatry also increases the level of violence and immorality. The Apostle Paul highlights this point in Romans, chapter one, verse 28: *Furthermore, since they did not think it worthwhile to retain the knowledge of God, he gave them over to a depraved mind; to do what ought not to be done.* Ever increasing idolatry and immorality affects every aspect of culture, including the Church. Left unchecked, the theologies and philosophies of our man-made idols insidiously work their way into the theology of the Church. This often leads to a denial of the divinity and necessity of Christ and his sacrifice, while at the same time, the violence and immorality of the culture intimidates and allures the Church away from *whatever is true, whatever is noble, whatever is right, whatever is pure, whatever is lovely, whatever is admirable...* (Philippians 4:8).

Stage Two: Faithful Leaders and Fervent Intercessors

As we read about the time of Elijah, when it seems as if God's people have been beaten and left on the ash-heap of history, a remnant prevails. Elijah's discouraged thinking in I Kings 19 is corrected by God's timely intervention at Mt. Horeb: *Yet I reserve seven thousand in Israel—all whose knees have not bowed down to Baal and all whose mouths have not kissed him.* The same is true during times of great awakening. The Lord preserves a remnant within His Church, led by spiritually mature Christians who faithfully preach and teach God's word unyieldingly.

rural and suburban neighborhoods become targets for crazed mass murderers, pedophiles, and armed robbers looking for a quick fix. What were once thought to be urban issues are no longer contained within the limits of our metropolitan areas. Today, as I write this introduction, I think of an elderly couple who were shot to death in their relatively "safe" suburban neighborhood, as their home was being robbed for drug money. The murderer showed no mercy.

Even rural neighborhoods are being infested with the residual by-products of our lifeless and godless society. Farm communities and rural towns have become epicenters for meth labs and marijuana gardens, planted deep within woods or cornfields. Where there once were neighborliness and a shared respect for the land and property of others, people are now fearfully arming themselves with stockpiles of guns and ammunition.

Yes, individual Christians are just beginning to experience and pay the toll of a society that laughs at the vulgar, idolizes the selfishly ambitious, desensitizes its children to indiscriminately kill (in a virtual world), applauds the lifestyles of the sexually immoral, and elevates feelings over truth and objectivity. The institutional church is also feeling the toll. Church leaders and parents are beginning to see more spiritual apathy and moral confusion among teens and young adults. Empty seats at worship and fewer children in Sunday school are setting off alarm bells in churches and denominational offices across the country.

What can be done to change society? What can churches do to attract the young and the spiritually apathetic? If history is any indicator, the Church has a choice to make, as it did during the period after the Revolutionary War. As we will see in this book, that period was arguably just as immoral and antichristian as is today's culture. Some of the churches in the 1780s and 1790s made accommodations, both in practice and in doctrine to become more "attractive," so that young and old alike would fill their pews once again and would hear messages that promoted "shared" values, based upon reasonable propositions. Other churches during that same time lost members, because they refused to compromise their doctrinal positions. They kept preaching and teaching the same historical Christian doctrines they had always taught. Eventually, within these churches, a small remnant of faithful pastors and members remained to teach their children God's truth and to live out His will in obedience to God. As they did, a renewed vision of God's present and future Kingdom permeated their hearts. That vision also broke their hearts, as the culture around them became increasingly dark. **It was during this part of "stage two" when they started to pray fervently.**

The question at the heart of this book is, "When will we in the 21st century begin to pray fervently?" More specifically, this book attempts to answer the question, "When will the Lord raise up a faithful remnant that finally realizes its dependency upon God and fervently prays for the next Great Spiritual Awakening?"

In the remaining pages of this book, I will attempt to answer that question. Based upon God's own word and God's historic work in the life of His Church, I want to suggest six answers to the question I have raised. The historical work is based upon my own research into awakening movements, particularly that of the Second Great Awakening. My prayer is that these answers will both challenge and encourage the Church to pray fervently and with great boldness for another such great awakening.

Terry D. Slachter

The Next Great Awakening

Day 1

Think about it!
Consider it! Tell us what to do!

Each year I read through the entire Bible from Genesis 1 to Revelation 22. Inevitably, the Lord brings to my attention some new insight or a new application for my life from verses I have read or even studied repeatedly over the years. There are some portions of Scripture I would prefer to skip. Two of them come readily to mind—Leviticus and the book of Judges.

Recently, I finished reading through the book of Judges. This book always leaves me discouraged. Here a triumphant and faithful generation passes away. This generation still remembered the taste of manna. They marveled at how the Lord dried up the Jordan River during the rainy season. Through the bold leadership of Joshua and Caleb, this generation conquered the giants in the land. How could the next generation—their children—so readily forget these national events? In just 40 years, which seems to be the Bible's length of time for a generation to pass away (see Numbers 14:29-35), they forgot all about the Lord and what He had done for Israel (Judges 2:10).

Perhaps we should not be surprised by this. Consider today's forty-somethings who were born in the 1970s. How many of these forty year olds remember, or even care to remember, how the Lord caused the Berlin Wall to fall and how the "iron curtain" melted away as the old Soviet Empire imploded? Generations of Americans prayed for that day to happen. There was always a lingering anxiety in the hearts of Americans that the Soviet Union might "push the button" and start WWIII. I can still remember the CD (Civil Defense) drills we went through in elementary school. To this day, I don't know why they made us hide underneath our desks. How could a desk save us from the radiation of a nuclear blast?

The point I'm making is that today's 40-year-olds never really experienced the emotional angst of the Cold War; therefore, it's not surprising that many don't remember the dates, names, or even reasons why the Berlin Wall came down. Without recording the historical facts and rehearsing the personal testimonies to the next generation, it should not surprise us how past events, no matter how significant, quickly fade away and become meaningless to succeeding generations.

The book of Judges tells us that the next generation knew neither the Lord, nor what He had done for the previous generations. Consequently, they turned to the gods of the people around them, provoking God's anger. A cycle of rebellion-retribution-repentance-and rescue becomes the outline of the book of Judges. With each cycle, God's people moved further and further away from the Lord, resulting in the gradual breakdown of civil authority and moral responsibility, with everyone doing whatever they saw fit to do in their own eyes. This plays out over the course of generations, until Israel reaches a new low toward the end of the book (chapters 19-20).

A New Sodom and Gomorrah?

When the men of Gibeah, from the tribe of Benjamin, were told that a Levite traveler and his "wife" (concubine) had entered the city and were staying at the home of an old man, they pounded on the man's door, demanding that he send out the Levite, so they could have sex with him. The old man refused, and instead he offered his own daughter and the Levite's wife to the perverse crowd of men. They refused this offer, and kept demanding that the old man send out the Levite. Finally, the

Levite pushed his wife out the door where the crowd raped and abused her through the night.

In the morning, the man's wife went back to the house where her "husband" was staying, and there she died at the threshold. The horrific and dehumanizing abuse she endured was a demonic mockery of God's concern for the stranger/alien (Lev. 19:33-34) and an insult to God who made man in His own image.

The Levite brought his wife back home and cut her remains into twelve parts, delivering a piece to every tribe of Israel. Everyone who saw it said, *Such a thing has never been seen or done, not since the day the Israelites came up out of Egypt.* Within the course of 200 years, the Israelites reached a new low of depravity—they became Sodom and Gomorrah.

The shock and the utter disgust over what had happened and what they were becoming sounded the alarm, **"Think about it! Consider it! Tell us what to do!"**

When God's people, in any age, reach this level of disgust, there is still room for hope.

Reflect upon these thoughts and pray.

Do you agree with the author's last statement?
If so, what would be the reason for that hope?

Lord, create a righteous and holy disgust in the hearts of your people. May they also cry out to you asking, "Tell us what to do!" Amen.

(Daily reading: Judges 19)

Day 2

The Jacobin Clubs

If you were a committed Christian living in the newly established United States of America, you would have experienced or read about many deplorable conditions which existed from the mid-1780s through the beginning decade of the 1800s. For example, families and entire communities were disintegrating because of alcoholism. During the Revolutionary War, the "softer" drinks, such as beer and wine, were scarce. Americans improvised and learned how to distill their own brand of rum (whiskey) during and after the war. In fact, Revolutionary soldiers were often given as much whiskey as they could drink. The result was a young nation of five million people, 300,000 of whom it was said, were drunkards.[1] Even President Adams' son Charles became an alcoholic, leaving a young wife and two young children destitute, while he disappeared into the dregs of society. Adams declared that his son was "a madman possessed of the devil."[2]

Alcoholism was a problem even within the Church. One man interviewed in a Boston newspaper claimed he could provide a list of over one hundred and twenty-three church deacons in Massachusetts who were drunks. He went on to say that of these one hundred twenty-three, forty-three of them became "sots." There was also a terrible drinking problem among pastors. The Rev. Leonard Wood claimed he knew of at least forty ministers in New England who drank excessively without apology.[3]

In addition to the drinking problem, America also faced a growing crime problem. As more people immigrated westward along the Ohio and

Tennessee Rivers, communities for hundreds of miles formed without any law. These areas quickly attracted gangs of robbers, murderers, horse thieves, counterfeiters, gamblers, and fugitives. When Peter Cartwright, the Methodist evangelist, settled down in Logan County, Kentucky, in 1793, the town was called "Rogues Harbor," because it contained fugitives from across the country who had fled from the law. These fugitives constituted a majority in the area, committing unspeakable acts of murder and robbery among the honest citizens. Their defiance of the law soon forced the law-abiding citizens to form their own militia, called "Regulators." Eventually, after a bloodbath between the two groups, the Regulators hunted down and lynched many of the surviving rogues.[4]

As bad as the drinking problem had become in the 1790s, and as lawless as the western territories were becoming in that same period, nothing shocked the sensibilities of Christian people of the day more than the Jacobin Clubs. These groups, many of whom were filled with young adults, were proliferating across the country as they sought to bring about the same kind of revolution that had taken place in France in 1789.

A "Paine" in the Barn

The name "Jacobin" came from the place where the leaders of the French Revolution met—the Dominican convent in Rue-Saint-Jacques in Paris. These leaders and their radical followers united into groups called "Jacobin Clubs" and were the initiators of the "Reign of Terror" that took place in France. The lower and middle classes of French society were particularly involved in rejecting the monarchy and freeing themselves from the abusive power of the Roman Catholic Church. While Americans were sympathetic with the French as allies in their own "Revolution," many of the Americans were unaware of the lawlessness and terror taking place within the new French Republic. They were also unaware of how the French Revolution was positioning itself to become a purely secular state, as both Protestant and Catholic clergy faced the guillotine.

The goddess of Reason was enshrined in Paris, as France removed all the public crosses (even crosses in cemeteries) and denounced Christianity as a superstition dangerous to liberty.

The sparks of the French Revolution soon floated all over Europe, igniting similar revolutions. These embers also crossed the Atlantic Ocean and landed on dry spiritual kindling, ripe for another revolution. The young and the disenfranchised people in America were especially vulnerable.

Thomas Paine, a fiery writer and leader for the American Revolution, was living in France during the French Revolution. He was a deist like many other notable revolutionary heroes such as Ethan Allen, who had captured Fort Ticonderoga; Thomas Jefferson; Henry Dearborn, and General Charles Lee. Soon the writings of Thomas Paine and French philosophers, such as Voltaire and Rousseau, were being printed in France and shipped to America for a penny a copy, or even given away.[5] The writings were not well-reasoned arguments in their opposition to Christianity; rather, they played to the prejudices, weaknesses, and passions of young people; people inclined to loose morals; the politically and socially disenfranchised; and people who already hated Christianity.

Within a few years, young people across the United States were reading Thomas Paine's, *Age of Reason*, as if it were the latest volume of the Harry Potter series. Some young people were even reading Paine's book behind their parents' backs, in their barns, as if it were contraband.[6]

As the new nation consolidated its power in a federal government, some of the states were finding it difficult to give up their autonomy and distinctiveness. There were also taxation issues, particularly Washington's whiskey tax, that became troublesome for the new federal government and for the adoption of its Constitution, which some viewed as a power grab by the federal government. All of these issues became dry kindling for the sparks of revolution that were flying across the Atlantic.

Soon American versions of the French Jacobin Clubs stirred up these resentments and raised suspicions about the federal government throughout the country, especially in places like Virginia, with its strong self-identity, and in the newer territories where there were few, if any, churches. Fiery leaders stirred up crowds as they preached against the federal government and against what they perceived as the "superstitions" of the Christian Church. Some groups stormed into church services, shouting vulgarities, and spitting on church members. Other groups, as the one described in the article below, were led by former Baptist preacher Elihu Palmer who wrote, *The simple truth is that their pretended Savior is nothing more than an illegitimate Jew. . .*[7]

The rhetoric of the Jacobin leaders and the writings of Thomas Paine and his French friends were threatening enough to worry even President John Adams. On April 25, 1799, he set aside a national day of prayer and fasting, declaring in his proclamation: *The most precious interests of the people of the United States are still held in jeopardy by the hostile designs and insidious acts of a foreign nation, as well as by the dissemination among them of those principles, subversive of the foundation of all religious, moral and social obligations that have produced incalculable mischief and misery in other countries.*[8]

Some may view President Adams' call for prayer as a political move in the light of an impending election against Thomas Jefferson later that year. However, the threat he cited in his proclamation was real. The American people were finally getting the troubling reports about the true nature of the French Revolution, and they were witnessing the fruit of it in their own communities, through the lives and actions of the Jacobin Clubs.

Abner Cunningham, who lived during this time, made a compelling case against the Jacobin Clubs in a report called, "Practical Infidelity Portrayed." Cunningham wrote about what actually happened to the young people who were caught up in the frenzy of a Jacobin Club in Orange County, New York.

They claimed the right to indulge in lasciviousness and to

recreate themselves as their propensities and appetites should dictate. "Those who composed this association," says the writer, "were my neighbors; some of them were my schoolmates. I knew them well, both before and after they became members. I marked their conduct, and saw and knew their ends. Their number was about twenty men and seven females. . . . Of these, some were shot; some hung; some drowned; two destroyed themselves by intemperance, one of whom was eaten by dogs, and the other by hogs; one committed suicide; one fell from his horse and was killed; and one was struck with an ax and bled to death. . . . Joshua Miller was a teacher of infidelity, and was shot off a stolen horse by Colonel J. Woodhull. N. Miller, his brother, was shot off a log while he was playing at cards on first-day morning, by Zebed June, in a scouting party for robbers. Benjamin Kelley was shot off his horse by a boy, the son of the murdered, for the murder of one Clarke; he lay above ground until the crows picked his bones. J. Smith committed suicide by stabbing himself while he was imprisoned for crime. W. Smith was shot by B. Thorpe and others, for robbery. S. T. betrayed his own confidential friend for five dollars; his friend was hung, and himself afterward was shot by D. Lancaster, said to be an accident. I heard the report of the gun and saw the blood. J. A. was shot by Michael Coleman, for robbing Abimel Young, in the very act. J. V. was shot by a company of militia. J. D., in one of his drunken fits, lay out, and was chilled to death. J. B. was hanged for stealing a horse. T. M. was shot by a Continental guard, for not coming to when hailed by the guard. C. S. was hung for the murder of Major Nathaniel Strong. J. Smith and J. Vervellon were hung for robbing John Sackett. B. K. was hung for stealing clothes. One other individual, hung for murder. N. B. was drowned, after he and J. B. had been confined for stealing a large ox sent to General Washington, as a present,

> by a friend. W. T. and W. H. were drowned. C. C. hung himself. T. F., Jun was shot by order of a court-martial for desertion. A. S. was struck with an ax, and bled to death. F. S. fell from his horse, and was killed. W. Clark drank himself to death; he was eaten by the hogs before his bones were found, and they were known by his clothing. He was once a member of respectable standing in the Presbyterian Church. While he remained with them, and regarded their rules and regulations, he was exemplary, industrious, sober, and respectable; and not until he became an infidel did he become a vagabond. His bones, clothing, and jug were found in a cornfield belonging to John Coffee, and they were buried without a coffin. J. A., Sen died in the woods, his rum-jug by his side. He was not found until a dog brought home one of his legs, which was identified by the stocking. His bones had been picked by animals. J. H., the last I shall mention in connection with that gang, died in a drunken fit. . . . The conduct of the females who associated with this gang was such as to illustrate its practical effects upon them. I shall only say that not one of them could or would pretend to know who the fathers of their offspring were. Perhaps hell itself could not produce more disgusting objects than were some of them."[9]

There were many in the 18th century Church, like Abner Cunningham, who were disgusted by what was happening in their culture, and it brought many to their knees in prayer. It was just one of the factors that led the faithful remnant to pray fervently for another awakening.

Reflect upon these thoughts and pray.

Are there groups, organizations or spheres of influence today whose beliefs, lifestyles, influences, or actions bring about such a repulsion in your heart that you can echo Abner Cunningham's sentiments, *Perhaps hell itself could not produce more disgusting objects than were (are) some of these?* Make a list of the things you find particularly "disgusting" in today's society and the reasons why.

Lord, I lift this list up to you today with compassion for those who are so blinded and deceived by the works of the evil one and the powerbrokers of this world. Free them by your truth and restore them by your grace. Amen.

(Daily reading: Romans 1:18-32)

Day 3

The Three Chained Women of Cleveland

The crescendo of present-day evils culminated with this statement: *Folks, how bad does it have to get, here in America, before we pray!* These were the fiery words of a sermon my Project Philip colleague and founder of Mission India, Dr. John DeVries, preached several years ago in the 1990s. John's passionate plea was rooted in his experiences with Hindu culture. Along with Dr. Erwin Lutzer, John co-authored a book entitled, Satan's Evangelistic Strategy for this New Age,[10] which documented the growing threat of the New Age movement to American culture. The book proved to be prophetic.

Based upon the Hindu teachings of pantheism (*God is all and all is God*) and reincarnation (*the transmigrating of souls after death*), the New Age movement Westernized these demonic lies to such a degree that today many people, even Christians, don't recognize how their own ideas, opinions and lifestyles are now being formed upon Hindu Philosophy. For example, the science and medical communities have so embraced yoga as a form of relaxation and stress reduction that according to Yoga Journal, 15.8 million Americans practice yoga on a regular basis. This is an 87% increase since 2004. The ultimate goal of yoga is self-realization and self-mastery over one's own body and over the material world. Practitioners of yoga become "absorbed" into a spiritual reality that transcends rational thought. In this, it is no different from mind-altering drugs and intoxication. The mind is numbed, and the will becomes pliable to any suggestion.

One other example of how far the New Age movement has mainstreamed in Western culture is in environmentalism. If everything is God, including nature, then man has lost his uniqueness as one made in the image of God. He is no different from the animals or a pine tree in the forest. So instead of man being the custodian over God's creation and using it for his own benefit, creation becomes equal to man, and man becomes subject to creation.

Let's take it one step further. If the universe is God, it must be perfect. If we are all gods, then we are all in charge of our own destinies in the universe. The only reason evil things happen, or disasters in nature harm us, is because we allowed them to hurt us. It is our fate. This absolves man from regrets, guilt and all responsibility for other people. As one New Age therapist said when asked about starving children, *What can I do if a child is determined to starve?*[11]

Is it any wonder then that in our country today there are so many disgusting acts of violence that dehumanize, especially the vulnerable in our society? Some prime examples follow. Millions of infants are aborted around the world, because they add to the depletion or pollution of the world's natural resources. There is senseless loss of life in schools and other public places perpetrated by terrorists or gunmen who shoot little children with the same callousness as they shoot video images in their video war games. The dehumanizing portrayal of women and children by the pornography "industry" creates a metastasizing cancer of human trafficking and heinous monsters, like Ariel Castro.

I thought we had seen it all in our day and age. But the account of Ariel Castro made me nauseous when the news first broke out of Cleveland, Ohio. Three women were kidnapped by Ariel Castro and chained as animals for over ten years; they were finally found and rescued in May of 2013. Castro kidnapped the three women as teenagers and chained them in his basement until he "broke their spirits," at which time, they were given access to the rest of the house.

During their ten-year imprisonment, Castro repeatedly raped all three women. He impregnated one of the women five times, and then he forced her to abort the babies by repeatedly punching her in her abdomen. Another woman gave birth to a baby girl, and, for reasons unknown, he permitted her to live.

I cannot begin to imagine the pain and suffering, both physically and emotionally, that these women and that little girl endured for over ten years! What possessed a man to treat these women like animals? He robbed them of their families, and he robbed them of the joys and celebrations of life. He robbed them of human dignity and respect. He even robbed them of any normal future, as they now have to deal with deep emotional and spiritual scars. His repulsive actions have created renewed fears in all parents and grandparents who wonder, "How many other monsters like Ariel Castro live in our cities?"

"Think about this! Consider it! Tell us what to do!"

Reflect upon these thoughts and pray.

What do you think is the source of or reason why our society has experienced so many heinous crimes and dehumanizing acts of violence against other human beings in the past twenty years? As a Christian, are you disgusted enough to start praying?

Is there a group in your church praying for the next awakening? If so, join with them and pray fervently for the Lord to pour out His Spirit upon the 21st century Church. If there is no such group in your church, ask the Lord to help you begin one and to lead others to join with you in regular prayer.

Lord, lead me and others in my church and community to gather regularly to pray for your Spirit to move with power in our nation. Amen.

(Daily reading: Genesis 18:16-33)

The Next Great Awakening

When will the Church Fervently Pray for it?

Answer:

When the Church Becomes Passionately Concerned for the Next Generation!

Day 4

Ichabod!

Sometimes I wonder what parents are thinking when they name their children. For instance, who would name their son "ESPN," or give their daughter the name "Xerox"? Yet, these two names, and many other product-based names, were given to children in the past few years. One wonders if these parents' motivation was money. *Hey, we named our son 'Orange-Jell-O'; he's a walking advertisement for your company! Shouldn't we be compensated?*

We may never know what possesses today's parents to give their children such unusual names, but we do know why the wife of Phinehas named her son Ichabod. The children of Israel went to battle against the Philistines during the time of the Judges. Eli was both judge and priest at the time, and his two rebellious sons, Hophni and Phinehas, also served (self-served would be more accurate) with their father as priests in the Tent of Meeting at Shiloh (I Sam. 2).

When the Israelites went to battle with the Philistine army, Israel's casualties were great—around 4000 men. They needed God's help, but instead of asking Eli to inquire of the Lord, they took matters into their own hands. Hophni and Phinehas took the Ark of the Covenant from behind the Tent of Meeting, and they carried the ark before the Israelite armies into battle. It was their way of trying to force or manipulate God's hand to victory. The plan backfired. God cannot be manipulated or treated as some lucky-charm. The Philistines stole the ark and promptly placed it in front of their idols as one of the spoils of war. The message they were sending was clear, *Our god is mightier than Jehovah!*

Not only was the ark captured, but the army of Israel was also decimated, and the two sons of Eli were killed on the battlefield. When the news of Israel's defeat and the ark's capture was made known, Eli fell backwards off his chair and died. The wife of Phinehas, who was dying due to a difficult labor and delivery, called her son "Ichabod," meaning, *the glory of the Lord has departed. It was her way of saying, I am fearful for Israel's future* (I Sam. 4:22). For Ichabod's mother, the ark represented God's throne and kingly presence in the midst of Israel. Without the Lord, Israel's prospects in the Promised Land looked bleak.

Poor Ichabod! Whenever someone used his name, it was a painful reminder of Israel's hopeless and glory-less situation. It was like new parents today naming their son "Foreclosure" after losing a home during the recession, or naming a daughter "911" to reflect the terrorist attacks on September 11, 2001. Ichabod's name reflected the final disappointing chapter in Israel's life as a people during the time of the Judges. When you thought Israel's depravity and spiritual condition could not sink much lower, here came Ichabod! His name said it all.

Reflect upon these thoughts and pray.

What are the things you fear most for today's younger generation? Are young adults leaving the Church? If so, why do you think they are?

Lord, I lift up this younger generation before you and ask that they may see, in their lifetime, your great reviving power move within the Church and within their culture. Amen.

(Daily reading: I Samuel 4:12-22)

Day 5

18th Century Animal House

The 1978 pop-culture classic "Animal House" was about a misfit group of college fraternity members who were academically-challenged and morally bankrupt in the 1960s. The only challenge they faced was the dean of their college who wanted to expel them all and close down their fraternity. Incidentally, the writers of this movie wanted to create a composite view of college life based upon their own supposed experiences. In so doing, they also managed to lampoon the hypocrisy of college administrators and college life.

What would an eighteenth century composite of college life or youth culture look like? Let us begin with Timothy Dwight's description.

Youths particularly, who had been liberally educated, and who with strong passions and feeble principles, were votaries of sensuality and ambition, delighted with the prospect of unrestrained gratification, and panting to be enrolled with men of fashion and splendor, became enamored of these new doctrines. [12]

If anyone understood youth culture in the late eighteenth and early nineteenth century, it was Timothy Dwight. Dwight was not only a pastor; he was also an educator, president of Yale College and a "traveling sociologist" who documented the life and culture of much of New England during this time.

Along with Dwight, others documented the eroding moral and spiritual character of youth culture in the 1790s. Some of this history comes from the students who lived through it and later chronicled it as pastors and college leaders. For example, at Williams College, Rev.

Jedidiah Bushnell recalled, *The French Revolution was very popular; while few of the students may have been in theory settled infidels, the great majority considered themselves deists and their morality was little better than their ideology.*[13] Thomas Robbins kept a diary of his time at Williams and described how the students formed "drinking companies" after their exams as a way to celebrate the conclusion of a school year. After the 1795-96 school year, Robbins wrote in his diary that the binge drinking and carousing was the worst "frolic" he had ever witnessed in his life. It was so bad that he wrote the following entry in his diary, *my feelings were exceedingly wounded by the carouse.*[14] Another Williams's student and the grandson of Jonathan Edwards, Timothy Woodbridge, wrote that the morality was decidedly low and that vices abounded, particularly gambling.[15] Williams College even held a mock celebration of *communion.*[16] Leverette Spring summarized the school's history at the end of the eighteenth century by listing only one underclassman as being a member of any church.[17]

Conditions were no better at Princeton. When Ashabel Green took over the presidency of the college in 1812, infidelity was rampant as the teaching of Thomas Paine spread through the college. Young men were fond of "novel speculations" and valued their own "genius." The students believed that any thought, doctrine or philosophy that was more than thirty years old was suspect and woefully outdated for the times. In open rebellion of Christianity, one student cut a rectangular cavity out of the chapel Bible and neatly inserted a deck of cards.[18] There was also a group of students living in Nassau Hall with "Jacobinic and anti-religious tenants" who proudly celebrated their infidelity in the face of the faculty by breaking into a local Presbyterian church and removing its pulpit Bible and then burning it.[19] When revival finally broke out in Princeton during the time of Dr. Green, Bibles were in such scarce supply that they had to be brought in from other cities to meet the demand.[20]

At Harvard College, Samuel Morrison reported that the typical Harvard student in the 1790s was an atheist.[21] The same was true at Dartmouth and Columbia in South Carolina, where in 1807, the students gathered on a cold February night to read from the works of Thomas Paine, sing French revolutionary songs, and chant until their voices became hoarse with the phrase, "Vive la Revolution!"[22]

The accounts of former students and faculty from Yale told of similar French revolutionary sympathies and devotion to deist authors such as Voltaire and Paine. Lyman Beecher wrote in his autobiography, *Most of the class before me were infidels, and called each other Voltaire, Rousseau, D'Alembert.*[23] Beecher also described Yale as an ungodly place where most of the students were skeptical about the Christian Faith and were more than happy to be free from its moral restraints. Many students kept wine and liquor in their rooms and profanity, gambling and all manner of licentiousness were common.[24] When Timothy Dwight became president of Yale in 1795, only one student from the entire student body, Shubael Bartlet, attended Dwight's first chapel service.[25] We also know that in that first academic year, there wasn't a single sophomore who professed to be a Christian, only one junior who made any profession, and eight or ten from the senior class who were communicant members.[26] There was even an incident in 1796 when students in the dining hall cut bread in pieces and with "unctuous mockery offered the elements to a solitary student who had just come from the table on communion Sunday."[27]

Compared to today's college life, collegiate life in the 1790s may seem normal or even tame by some standards. Keep in mind: 1) Many of these students were very young, ages 14-17. 2) Most of these students came from homes of either privileged or educated parents who expected their children to become leaders in government, law, business, science, and even ministry. 3) Divinity students would normally attend these colleges before they apprenticed with a local pastor. There was already a shortage of pastors to fill the pulpits of existing churches in New England, not to mention, a huge need for pastors to move westward and begin ministries among young pioneers.[28] By 1800, nearly one million people had left the East for Ohio and beyond.[29] 4) These colleges were, for the most part, "church-owned" and historically "Christian" in their world and life views. There were few alternatives. In fact, Thomas Jefferson had strongly urged William and Mary College in Virginia to become the nation's first truly secular college. Jefferson wrote, *The College must free men from superstition, not inoculate them with it.*[30] He went on to call for the abolishment of the professorship of divinity.

Spiritual darkness was quickly engulfing American youth culture. To many Christians living in the 1790s, the future leaders of the country and Church looked no more impressive than Hophni and Phineas.

Reflect upon these thoughts and pray.

Do you think college campuses in the United States are more secular or more hostile to the Christian Faith than in the 1790s? Do you have children or grandchildren who are or will be going to college? What are your greatest concerns for them? Lift them up to the Lord in prayer.

(Daily reading: I Samuel 1:21-28)

Day 6

Mrs. Judson's Tears

Adoniram Judson was only three years old when his mother began to teach him how to read. One day, after being away from the family, Adoniram's father, the Rev. Adoniram Judson, returned to find his first-born son reading an entire chapter from the Bible. This greatly pleased a father who had very high expectations for his son. The Rev. Judson was no easy man to please. He was once described as a "man of inflexible integrity and uniform consistency of Christian character."[31] One person described him as a cross between a Hebrew patriarch and a Roman censor.[32]

Young Judson was precocious, independent and bright. He loved to read, and when a neighbor would not loan him a new book that had been recently published on the subject of the Apocalypse, he went home and cried to his father. The senior Judson promised him that from that point on, he would have as many books as he could read. Adoniram was only eleven years old.

After a period of severe sickness, which curtailed his studies and brought him to the point of near death at the age of fourteen, Adoniram gave serious thought to his future plans. Before his sickness, he ambitiously dreamed of being an orator, or a statesman, or even a poet. He wanted to be famous and to accomplish great things that would be remembered long after his death. His near-death experience sobered his thinking about worldly, fleeting fame. He concluded that the work his father was doing as a Congregational minister had great merit, both for this world and for the world to come. He was also painfully aware that his heart was full of selfish ambition and vanity.

At the age of sixteen, Adoniram entered Providence College (later named Brown University) one year in advance of the normal age for college enrollment, and there he excelled in all of his classes. He graduated at the age of nineteen as valedictorian of his class. The college president was so smitten by the young man's academic achievements and conduct in college that he sent a personal letter to Adoniram's father. He ended the letter with this salutation, *and I most heartily pray that the Father of mercies may make him now, while a youth, a son in his spiritual family and give him an earnest of the inheritance of the saints in high.*[33] Little did the president of the college know that during his college years, he had become a deist.

During the course of his studies, the French Revolution had its impact upon many students as a "sprit" of skepticism, guised as liberty, pervaded college campuses. In some colleges, even the faculty conspired against the traditional orthodox teachings of the Church, raising questions in the minds of students, questions that some were not even asking. Some students on college campuses were calling each other "Voltaire" or "Rousseau" after the men who were the heroes of the movement leading up to the French Revolution. For the young and inquiring mind of Adoniram Judson, the "spirit" was too beguiling. Without a spiritual and intellectual giant to combat the spirit of skepticism at Brown, as there was at Yale with Timothy Dwight, Adoniram Judson fell prey to every Christian parent's worst fear—a bad and misleading friend.

Adoniram developed a friendship with an upperclassman by the name of Jacob Eames. Eames, it turned out, was a rabid deist, and soon his influence upon the younger man took its toll. Adoniram soon confessed that he, too, was a deist. Together, Jacob and Adoniram were making ambitious plans to begin a law practice or to write dramatic plays so that they could become famous.

After college, Adoniram opened up a private academy at Plymouth where he taught for two years, before he decided to close the school and travel around New England, especially New York, where the newly invented steam ship was in harbor. Before he set out, he decided to "come out of the closet" about his deism.

Adoniram's father dealt with the news in typical New England fashion—he severely attacked every argument Adoniram posed against orthodox theology, citing traditional Church teachings. Underneath every response was the pain of a hurting and disappointed father. Adoniram's mother shared this pain. While she said very little, she wept bitterly and prayed.

When Adoniram finally took leave of his parents, he thought that his infidelity was superior to his father's arguments, but as he later admitted, he had no defense against his mother's tears which would haunt him long after this confrontation.[34]

Reflect upon these thoughts and pray.

Do you think the 21st century Church is weeping bitterly and praying fervently for these young people just as Mrs. Judson did for her son? Is there a young person in your family or in your church who has recently "come out of the closet," admitting his or her departure from the Christian Faith or the Christian view of morality? Pray fervently for that young person and his or her parents. Ask the Lord to change his or her heart.

(Daily reading: Psalm 126)

Day 7

Mainstream

A common question I often hear today in churches within the greater evangelical church community is, *Where are the young adults?* The twenty somethings (often called "mosaics") are not attending or getting involved in any church. They leave the church youth group, attend college, and are never heard from again. Are these young people simply attending other churches with bigger and better post-high groups and ministries or, is it even worse than that? Have they left the Christian Faith altogether?

Researchers like David Kinnamon, who is the president of the Barna Group, have been studying this issue and interviewing many of these young people who no longer attend church. He wrote in his book, *You Lost Me, The ages eighteen to twenty-nine are the black hole of church attendance; this segment is "missing in action" from most congregations. Overall, there is a 43 percent drop-off between the teen and early adult years in terms of church engagement. These numbers represent about eight million twenty somethings who were active churchgoers as teenagers but who will no longer be particularly engaged in a church by their thirtieth birthday.*[35]

Kinnamon also found that among young people raised in the Church, *many have favorable views of Jesus, but they also harbor significant doubts about the central figure of Christianity. Young adults are more likely than any other age group to believe that Jesus sinned, to doubt the miracles Jesus performed, and to express skepticism about his resurrection.*[36] He also found skeptism among this generation concerning the reliabilty of orginal biblical manuscripts. They tend to read the Bible through a lens of pluralism; *their changing media behaviors and vanishing attention spans make the physical medium of Scripture less viable; and they seem less likely than previous generations to believe the Scriptures have a claim on human obedience.*[37]

At a conference that I recently attended featuring David Kinnamon, he encouraged churches to view these young adults as being in one of three categories: nomads, prodigals, or exiles. Nomads are spiritual wanderers who are not particularly committed anywhere and can easily drift in and out of the Church. Prodigals are young people who have decidely left the Christian Faith, either becoming agnostic or following some other religion or spiritual leader outside of orthodox Christianty. Exiles are modern day Daniels, trying to live and make a difference in Babylon. They are thrown into politcial, social, economic, or educational institutions and are told to leave their faith and morality back in "Israel" and learn the way and language of Babylon. They want and need the spiritual support of the Church community. They even believe that the Christian Faith has something to offer for their fellow Babylonians. However, they are not finding the needed support in many churches. Either too much of Babylon has entered the Church, or too many tears are shed by the rivers of Babylon, remembering only the past, while the "songs of Zion" need to be sung and played in this foreign land (Psalm 137).

My growing concern is not only for today's twenty-somethings, but it is also for the children coming into this world. What was discouraged, considered unpopular, or even banned twenty years ago have all now become mainstream in our society. We laugh at jokes and watch T.V. programs and movies that a few years ago people would not have found humorous and, frankly, would have been greatly offended by had they witnessed it then. Now extrapolate what the next twenty years will bring if things do not change.

I was painfully reminded of that recently while spending time with my two-year-old grandson, Kaleb. Grampa was trying to get him to take his afternoon nap, to no avail. Finally, we went into the family room and sat on the recliner to watch something on television that might relax him enough to make him fall asleep. As you may have already guessed, Grampa quickly relaxed and fell asleep, while wide-awake Kaleb gave his blankey and favorite teddy bear to his snoring grampa. But before I fell asleep, he and I watched an episode of Bonanza. This show had been taped when I was a kid, and I was amazed at the civility and morality of that show compared to today's standards. When two of the Cartright boys stumbled across a woman bathing in a lake, with red-faced embarassment, they quickly turned their heads until the young woman had gotten dressed. Now compare that with what I stumbled upon one evening at 8:00 PM while channel surfing. The CBS show was called, Two Broke Girls, and it featured two waitresses. In this particular episode, the one young woman was waiting upon a table with two men who were trying to ask her out. Their conversation was vulgar enough to make a sailor blush. Perhaps the most morally offensive part of the show, however, was to hear the sounds of her waitress friend having sex in a storeroom of the resturaunt.

I thought that the eight to nine o'clock evening hour was still considered to be a "family hour" for televison programing. If this is the new norm, then I dread to think what my grandson's generation will be watching as entertainment in the next twenty years, unless things drastically change.

As Christians we can capitulate, declaring today's culture "the new norm" and strive to endure it the best way we can, retreating into "Christian fox-holes" until Christ returns. Or, we can begin to pray fervently for the Lord to move and transform this culture, so that today's babies can grow up in a world where they may experience a taste of Christ's just and righteous Kingdom.

This kind of cultural transformation always begins with the reformation of Christ's Church. The only way the Church can be reformed is through the power of the Holy Spirit. He will raise up a remnant within the Church who believe that the Church needs to be awakened, and who will fervently pray for it to happen.

Reflect upon these thoughts and pray.

Are you fearful for the next generation? If so, begin praying for the Spirit to awaken the 21st century Church, beginning with your own church. Ask the Lord to give your pastor(s) power in preaching and teaching God's word. Also, ask the Lord to impress upon their hearts the urgent need to pray fervently for a great awakening of the Church.

Consider forming a prayer group in your church or within your local Christian community for the younger generation who have walked away from the Christian Faith. This group should also pray for college students who face challenges to their faith as they leave their nurturing homes and church enviroments.

(Daily reading: Psalm 78:1-8)

The Next Great Awakening

Day 8

The Broken Down Altars

King Ahab has gone down in biblical history as the one who did *more evil in the eyes of the Lord than any of those before him . . ..and did more to provoke the Lord, the God of Israel, to anger than did all the kings before him* (I Kings 16:30, 33). Now that's quite a statement, especially when you consider what the Lord had told Jeroboam, the first king of the ten northern tribes, *You have done more evil than all who lived before you. . .* (I Kings 14:9). Ahab's infamy even surpassed the man who had first introduced a pagan symbol for the Lord (a golden calf) and mass-produced it in convenient locations to keep the people from worshipping the true God of Israel in the city of Jerusalem.

So what did Ahab do to earn such a reputation? I Kings 16:31-34 records four things, and the author will go on to describe two more in succeeding chapters. First, Ahab went far beyond Jeroboam who had "paganized" the worship of the Lord. Ahab tried to expunge every aspect of Jehovah God from the life of Israel. He broke down every altar dedicated to the worship of the Lord; he even allowed his wife to "kill-off" all the prophets of the Lord (I Kings 18:4).

The Bible records that Ahab married Jezebel, the daughter of Ethbaal, for political reasons. Like his father, who wanted to align Israel into a closer relationship with all of the Canaanite nations near it, Ahab married the daughter of Sidon's influential leader. From a political perspective, it made sense. From the Lord's perspective, Ahab was declaring his complete independence from Him. By his actions, he might as well have spoken these words: *Who needs the Lord for protection when threatened; I have close political alliances with other nations? Together, we can muster huge armies to ward off any threat or to intimidate Jerusalem to the south!* The alliance with Sidon was even more offensive, because it was the "birthplace" of Baal worship.

Ahab's marriage to Jezebel led to a third "reputation-builder" when Ahab allowed his wife to make Baal worship a matter of court policy. He no longer merely tolerated Baal worship in Israel, but he actively promoted it by building a temple to Baal in the heart of his capital. This act was a defiant mockery of the temple of the Lord, which was located in the center of Jerusalem. Jezebel even went so far as to introduce witchcraft and other forms of occult worship into the land (II Kings 9:22). Under Ahab's "leadership," Israel became a demonic cesspool.

Finally, Ahab's depraved nature seems to have had no limits when he defied God's word and permitted Hiel to rebuild the city of Jericho—something expressly prohibited by the Lord in Joshua 6:26. When he coveted Naboth's vineyard, robbed this man of his life, and took his family's land of inheritance in Israel (I Kings 21), Ahab demonstrated a callous heart toward human life. The heart of Ahab was so hardened against the Lord that he no longer feared the word of the Lord nor respected the value and dignity of human life. Yet, the Lord's mercy and grace were about to shine through the gloom of Ahab's Israel. Even in a culture as demonic and depraved as Israel was during the reign of Ahab and Jezebel, we see God at work.

Glimmers of Light in the Darkness

Schools of the Prophets existed during this time. These schools were also present during the time of Samuel (I Samuel 10:10) and even during the time of the Prophet Isaiah (Isaiah 8:16). The school of the Prophets were likely communities of people who remained faithful to the Lord during times of spiritual barrenness and idolatry. The students in these schools looked to God's faithful prophets for leadership and wisdom as they encouraged each other and the other seven thousand in Israel whose knees have not bowed down to Baal and all whose mouths have not kissed him (I Kings 19:18). The Lord always preserves a remnant in such times.

It required drastic measures to rebuild the broken down altars of the Lord in a land where they were prohibited and forgotten. It was in this context that the Lord sent his prophet Elijah to announce to Ahab that there would be such a severe famine in the land that there would be neither dew nor rain in the next few years except at MY word (I Kings 17:1). As the Israelites were suffering, the Lord sent Elijah to his own private stream with "raven-waiters" to bring him food to eat. When that stream dried up, the Lord sent Elijah to the very birthplace of Baal worship—Zarephath of Sidon. Here he stayed with a widow and her young son—the very neediest family in the land. Here the Lord provided an abundance of bread for the prophet and his host.

All of this is dripping with irony. It is as if the Lord is saying to His people: Why do you put your trust in Baal, a fertility god who is supposed to provide bread and yet is unable to do so year after year, even in his own back yard, while My prophet has plenty of water and food? In fact, the Lord even provided for Elijah and his host in Jezebel's own homeland—the very birthplace of Baal worship. In one of the darkest periods of Israel's history God; raised up a faithful remnant, sent in a fiery prophet, and demonstrated his tough love with a famine. All three divine actions became the prerequisites before God's glory was revealed on Mt. Carmel.

Reflect upon these thoughts and pray.

Were there other times in Church history when God raised up a faithful remnant during a time of spiritual barrenness? Do you think God is raising up "schools of the prophets" today? If so, where are they?

Lord, raise up a faithful remnant of people across this nation who will fervently pray for the next great awakening and who will faithfully teach and preach Your word without compromise. Amen.

(Daily reading: I Kings 18:1-15)

Day 9

Darkness Covers the Land

The Lord warned the Israelites to keep their covenant with Him or they would face *sudden terror, wasting diseases and fever that will destroy your sight and drain away your life* (Lev.26:16). In the 1790s, the United States faced two devastating diseases that seemed to come right out of the pages of the Bible. Yellow fever was an urban killer. Symptoms of this disease are fevers, chills, nausea, muscle pain and anorexia. In the toxic phase of the disease, damage occurs to the liver, causing the skin to appear a jaundiced yellow color. This phase leads to increased bleeding and death.

The second disease was smallpox. Smallpox appears in the blood vessels of the skin, mouth and throat. On the skin, the smallpox rash becomes fluid-filled blisters. The long-term complications of smallpox are deforming scars on the face and body, limb deformities and blindness caused from ulcers that develop in the cornea. Before the development of a vaccine in 1796, this disease killed millions of people around the world. It is estimated that three and a half million Mexicans died of smallpox when the Spaniards entered the New World,.

These two dreaded diseases afflicted thousands of Americans in the 1790s, as documented below.[38]

1792	Boston (small pox)
1793	Vermont (putrid fever and influenza)
1793	Virginia (influenza killed 500 people in 5 counties)
1793	Philadelphia (yellow fever took the lives of 4000 people)

1793	Harrisburg, PA (many unexplained deaths)
1794	Philadelphia (yellow fever)
1796-98	Philadelphia (yellow fever)
1803	New York (yellow fever)

In addition to these diseases, there were threats of terror from Indian tribes, depraved fugitives from the law, and enemy agents from Europe sent to deprive the United States of its valuable fur trade. The Indians massacred entire families, burning homes and crops, often in retaliation for brutal acts of barbarism committed against them by lawless white men.

The problem was so great that in 1800, congress reported that in the Northwest Territory (Ohio, Illinois, Michigan, and Indiana):

> There has been one court having cognizance of crimes in five years; and the immunity which offenders experience attracts, as to an asylum, the most vile and abandoned criminals, and at the same time deters useful and virtuous persons from making settlements in such society. This territory is exposed, as a frontier, to foreign nations, whose agents can find sufficient interest in exciting or fomenting insurrection and discontent, as thereby they can more easily divert a valuable trade in furs from the United States.[39]

If disease and terror didn't alarm people living in the 1790s, the young nation's financial outlook would have, because it was just as sobering; pirates were terrorizing American ships on the high seas, there were trade embargos in Europe, and debts to other nations were mounting. With so much suffering and fear within the young nation, some were beginning to ask, *Is this the hand of God's Judgment?* When people looked at the death toll in Philadelphia, the nation's capital city in the 1790s, many wondered if God were not making His displeasure known to the leaders of this nation.

Reflect upon these thoughts and pray.

Do you think God is making His displeasure of the United States known today? If so, in what ways? Does God judge the nations of the world? If so, how and for what purpose?

Lord, with every crisis or tragedy our nation faces, may it remind us both of our dependence upon You for all things, and that there are painful consequences for nations that turn their back away from You and Your word. Amen.

(Daily reading: Psalm 82)

Day 10

9/11

Isaiah the prophet spoke a word of judgment against the nations of the earth, but his strongest warnings targeted God's own people. Over the centuries the Christian Church has cherished many of Isaiah's comforting prophesies, especially the ones about Christ, while callously ignoring both the dire warnings to the nations and to the remnant of Judah. As Brian Edwards writes in his book, Revival,

We can say the same of Peter's warning in chapter 4 of his first letter, *For it is time for judgment to begin at the household of God; and if it begins with us, what will be the outcome for those who do not obey the gospel of God (ESV)?* Isn't it true that we often gloss over the biblical teachings, in both the Old and New Testaments, which remind us that God refines His people and even disciplines His Church if they fail to discipline themselves, *Those whom I love, I reprove and discipline, so be zealous and repent* (Revelation 3:19).

God's people, in every age, have been quick to point fingers, blaming the world (non-Christians) for all of the evil and moral darkness in society. The Church is also quick to become judge and jury when a natural or man-made disaster strikes anywhere in the country, indicting the evil power brokers of culture as being culpable for inducing God's wrath against us.[41] While it is true that God judges the nations of the earth, and that the sins of any people are a disgrace, the Church must also humbly acknowledge its complicity in that disgrace. God's people should respond to national tragedies and to the growing moral darkness of the culture with the prayer that David offered at the end of Psalm 139, *Search me (us) O God, and know my (our) heart; test me (us) and know my (our) anxious thoughts. See if there is any offensive way in me (us), and lead me (us) in the way everlasting.*

After the tragic loss of life on 9/11 and the subsequent fear of more terror attacks, many people sought comfort by gathering together in churches across the country. I was a pastor in a church in Dearborn, Michigan, at the time. There was heightened concern in this city, because it has one of the largest populations of Arab-Americans in the entire country. Many Arab-Americans were afraid of reprisals and had placed American flags in the windows of their businesses. Everyone else in the city anxiously wondered if there were al-Qaeda-type cells in our own backyards. Perhaps my most poignant memory was keeping the church open every day for prayer. In that first week, many came and quietly prayed for the nation, and for the many victims. It was also a time for soul-searching. One woman I talked to was so frightened every time she heard an airplane fly over her house in the subsequent days, that she could not sleep at night. She was afraid for her children. She was afraid of her own mortality, even as a Christian.

As I referenced earlier, many in the greater evangelical world are quick to point fingers every time disaster strikes. Could God be trying to get the attention of His Church when the nation faces tragedy? Is the Lord pointing His finger at the Church. Is the Lord pointing His finger at the church because we have not faithfully maintained the "alters of the Lord" in our homes, churches, and personal lives? And are we experiencing trouble in the land because the Church fears the moniker "Troubler"? (1 Kings 18:17) I tend to agree with Dr. Erwin Lutzer who wrote in a 1986 Moody Monthly article:

> It's popular to blame the Supreme Court, the humanists, and radical feminists for our country's eroding standards of decency and growing disrespect for human life. But the responsibility might more properly be laid at the feet of those who know the living God, but have failed to influence society. If we were few in number, we might evade the blame, but there are tens of thousands of evangelical congregations

and several million born-again believers in America. Yet we continue to lose crucial battles. Perhaps the church doesn't suffer for the sins of the world as much as the world suffers for the sins of the church.[42]

Reflect upon these thoughts and pray.

Do you think the Lord is displeased with today's Church? If so, what needs to change in our churches? Make this a matter of prayer as you pray for your own church.

(Daily reading: Matthew 5:13-16)

Day 11

A Famine of the Word

When we read about God's judgments in the Bible, the list includes famine, pestilence, devastating diseases, enemy attacks, earthquakes, and Egyptian-style plagues like frogs, gnats, and darkness. In the book of Amos, there is a judgment far worse than all of these more familiar signs of God's displeasure. The prophet Amos brings a message of warning to God's people who, after tasting the fruits of God's blessings, did not reciprocate that love or faithfulness to God. Instead, they abused the poor and widows, gloated with pride over their wealth and security, while dabbling with the idols of the nations around them. Yes, they brought their sacrifices to the Lord, but they were repulsive in God's eyes as their religious practices and words did not match the way they lived their lives. The prophet warned them that they were ripe for God's judgment, and the Lord sent a famine of food and water (4:6-8) that brought about belated results. In fact, their entire society was rotting from within. J. A. Motyer in his book entitled, *The Day of the Lion,* draws this conclusion about what happened in Israel, and continues to happen, when a people does not heed God's judgments.

> When we see society opening at the seams, old bonds weakening, old norms relaxing, old absolutes rejected, when we see the human person not as able as hitherto to stand the strains of life and there are more breakdowns, more suicides, God is telling man, collectively and individually, that life apart from Him is not possible, that inherited spiritual capital drains away and, left to himself, man becomes progressively unable to cope.[43]

In chapter 8:11, Amos went on to warn the Israelites of an even greater, more severe famine. "The days are coming," declares the Sovereign Lord, "when I will send a famine through the land—not a famine of food or a thirst for water, but a famine of hearing the words of the Lord." This famine would be a more devastating judgment than a crop failure or drought. The Prophet warned of a time when the word would either become scarce or the Lord would intentionally mute His own words to them so they would be . . . *ever hearing, but never understanding* (Isaiah 6:9). The result of this famine would cause men to *stagger from sea to sea and wander from north to east, searching for the word of the Lord, but they will not find it* (Amos 8:12). Even the next generation of young men and women would faint because of this thirst for the word, as they would search from sea to sea for the latest new religion or spiritual experience (8:13). Eventually, their search for that which they once had, and so lightly regarded, would draw them into the cults of other peoples. They would seek out many gods to fill the vacuum, only to discover that what was offered would never truly satisfy their hunger and thirst (8:14).

Jesus wept over the sight of Jerusalem whose people were living as sheep without a shepherd. The religious leaders of the day were creating a famine of the word, even as the Word Incarnate was present among them. *Woe to you experts in the law, because you have taken away the key to knowledge. You yourselves have not entered, and you have hindered those who were entering* (Luke 11:52). While the religious leaders were ever hearing but never

> *I lately attended public worship upon the Sabbath, in neighboring town. The minister preached a very serious and good sermon, and appeared to feel the importance of what he said; but many of the hearers, especially of the young people, were very inattentive, and some of them very rude. O, how did I wish some word spoken by the preacher, might reach their consciences, and some arrow prick their hearts, check their levity and make them serious. To see a minister spending his strength for naught, and young people trifling and playing in the house of God, gave me very disagreeable feelings; and if my heart does not deceive me, I wish all may be saved.*
>
> *A testimony of a new Christian given to Rev. Samuel Waterman, of Plymouth, Conn. 1799*

understanding... *for this people's heart has become calloused; they hardly hear with their ears, and they have closed their eyes* (Math.13:14-15), there were others whose hearts burned within them when they heard the Word Incarnate (Luke 24:32). There was not a famine of the word, only a famine of "hearing" the word of God.

In the eighteenth century, there was also a famine of hearing the word of God. Many pulpits were passionless, and in some cases, Christless. Even in churches where the gospel was preached with passion, authority, and integrity, there was a famine of the word. Hearts became hardened under the preaching of God's word. In some cases, people mocked the pastors who still believed and preached the infallibility of God's word, the atonement of Christ, and the Trinity. Is that same callousness of heart taking place within our churches today? If so, is this a sign of God's displeasure towards the 21st century Church?

B.A.D.D

As one who has been preaching in churches for over 25 years, I can honestly say that preaching has become more difficult in the last ten years. What I mean by *difficult* is that the attention span for the word of God is at an all-time low. Many have argued that it is not a spiritual or biblical issue as much as it is a sociological or even a physiological one, especially with people under 25 years of age. Preaching gurus and college and seminary professors suggest that this is the new norm, and that preachers today just need to adapt and use whatever rhetorical and/or audio-visual technology is available in the preacher's arsenal to make the best of it. Still others suggest using a more avant-garde approach to preaching and teaching, whereby the preacher acts as a discussion facilitator and allows everyone to give his or her own opinion of what the Bible teaches or what they think God is saying to them at the moment. This avoids any personal offense or any politically incorrect verbiage and plays well with the younger set, who does not like to hear, Thus saith the Lord! One other popular approach today is to choreograph the entire worship service, from offering handsome preachers to providing concert-style worship groups that produce weekly performances that rival anything on television. State-of-the-art facilities, acoustics, lighting, celebrity appearances, and even a coffee shop for intermissions during the offering are all part of the accoutrements surrounding a fifteen-minute talk that is polished, entertaining, and contains only 1%-milk content.

Please do not misunderstand me. I am not opposed to audio/visual technology, good acoustics or even state-of-the-art facilities. My point is that we are doing everything in our own strength and power to capture the attention of young people and adults who do not seem to suffer from this same "attention deficit" problem at football stadiums, rock or country music concerts, or even in a college calculus class. The real problem is a Biblical Attention Deficit Disorder—a sickness of the soul that only the Spirit can heal. The 21st century Church cannot create a spiritual hunger or thirst for God or His word, especially when hearts are consumed with idols, as in the days of Amos. Instead of trying to compensate for this lack of attention, considering it the new normal for this generation, the Church should discern whether this is a sign of His displeasure. When children and young people in the Church do not have a hunger for God's word, this is a judgment upon the Christian community, because you . . . commanded the prophets not to prophesy (Amos 2:12), and because you . . . *are complacent in Zion . . . and you feel secure on Mount Samaria* (Amos 6:1).

Without true spiritual revival in the Church, the result will be what Paul forewarned in II Timothy 4:3-4: For the time will come when men will not put up with sound doctrine. Instead, to suit their own desires, they will gather around them a great number of teachers to say what their itching ears want to hear.

Reflect upon these thoughts and pray.

Do you attend church or Bible studies with a hunger for God's word? If not, ask the Lord to discern your heart and show you what idol(s) is/are consuming your time and attention.

Lord I lift up my pastor(s) as they preach and teach from week to week. Give them power and clarity of mind and voice to preach your word with authority and passion. Protect them and their families from the evil one, and from the temptation to compromise with the world in order to be popular or relevant. Amen.

(Daily reading: Amos 8:7-14)

Consider beginning a prayer group, or join an existing prayer group that meets on Saturday or early Sunday morning for the express purpose of praying for your pastor, Sunday school teachers and all who preach and teach God's word.

Day 12

Scientology and the Crucifix

Children are the most vulnerable during times of famine. Their bloated stomachs and emaciated bodies crying for food pierce the hearts of their parents who are helpless to do anything to relieve their hunger. These sights ought to pierce the hearts of all humanity. But, as we read in yesterday's devotion, there is a far more deadly type of famine that strikes both young and old—a famine of the word. Amos warned God's people in Amos 8:11 that a time was coming when there would be a famine of hearing the word of God, when people would suffer from God's righteous judgment, when God's word would either not be available to them or they would not be able to hear it and comprehend it. As a result, they would search from sea to sea to find comfort and hope. Their search would bring them to cults and other false religions, wandering from idol to idol for spiritual food and water. This spiritual hunger is God's judgment on a proud and rebellious people who refuse to repent and seek the Lord with all of their hearts.

We pointed out in yesterday's devotion that there is a famine of the word even in the Church today. A growing attention deficit with God's word is a sign of God's judgment, beginning with the household of faith. God's people need to look at their own hearts and priorities. But what about the greater culture? Is there a famine of God's word extending beyond the household of faith? If the signs of this kind of famine are: people staggering from sea to sea, north to east, searching, but not finding God's word; young men and women fainting and dying (taking their own lives) for lack of spiritual food and drink; and finally, people running to every possible idol, cult, guru, or spiritual fad to find hope, we can declare that there is a famine of the word today in this country!

Exhibit A

I have never understood why anyone would believe in a religious movement founded by a science fiction writer. This is the case in the United States today. Science fiction writer, L. Ron Hubbard, founded Scientology in 1953, and it now claims 3.5 million adherents around the world. While these numbers may be exaggerated, the thought that anyone would believe Hubbard's ideas to be credible proves the prophetic truth of Amos 8:12-14: *Men will stagger from sea to sea and wander from north to east, searching for the word of the Lord, but they will not find it. . .* (So they will search for other gods and) *swear by the shame of Samaria, or say, "As surely as your god lives. . ."*

Scientology believes that the way man finds freedom from fear and peace for the soul is by having its members consciously re-experience painful or traumatic events in their past to free themselves from their hindering effects. At the heart of their "theology" is the belief that the human soul is alien in origin, and has lived on other planets. The soul (thetan) reincarnates repeatedly in different forms, collecting multiple painful traumas from life to life.

Why would anyone turn away from the true source of peace, hope and ultimate redemption that Christ offers, to run after one man's fiction? As Christians, we ask, *Why haven't these people looked to God's word for hope?* Has the Lord closed their ears, or is there a famine of hearing the word, because the Church isn't fulfilling its great commission to sow the seed of the gospel extravagantly, as in the parable of the sower (Matthew 13), and with prayerful simplicity and clarity (Col.4:4)? Could it be that the 21st century Church is only planting the seed of the gospel in church buildings, and not out in the fields where wise farmers plant their seeds?

There is a sad irony within today's Christian Church. We do a great deal of good around the country, such as feeding the poor, helping out after disasters, and providing clothes and school supplies to children who need them. All of these deeds have their place and are worthy of doing. But, while we are doing these many good things for others, we often forget or have few resources left over, to sow the seed of the gospel to these same people. Often doing only the bare minimum, we pass out a few New Testaments and consider our work done.

Exhibit B

I live near Grand Rapids, Michigan, and our ministry is located in this Midwestern city. People know Grand Rapids for its many churches, seemingly one on every corner, and as of late, they also know it as the home of the Grand Rapids Art Prize. This international venue for art and artists has drawn thousands of people into the city, either to compete for a cash prize with their latest masterpiece or to view all of the art exhibits staged throughout the city. Three years ago, the top prize went to an artist who depicted Jesus on the cross. When a third-grade class of students from one of the local public schools took in some of the art pieces, their teacher, a Christian woman, asked her students to interpret that year's top prize winner—the crucifix. To this teacher's surprise, none of the students in her class had any idea what the picture was about. One little boy attempted a guess: *He looks like some guy laid out from a motorcycle accident.*

These children had no idea who Jesus was or what he was doing on a cross. While these children did not have bloated bellies or emaciated bodies, they showed signs of a different kind of famine in the land. Their ignorance of Jesus should pierce the hearts of every Christian.

Reflect upon these thoughts:

If, in the United States, there are thousands of children who know nothing about Jesus and why He suffered on the cross, what does this say about the priorities of the 21st century Church? What are you and your church doing in your neighborhood or city to introduce Jesus to every household?

Lord, give the churches of the United States a passion to sow the seed of your word in every household in this country. Give every girl and boy an opportunity to hear the good news of Jesus. Amen.

(Daily reading: Romans 10:8-15)

The Next Great Awakening

Day 13

Rebuilding the Broken Altars

God instructed Elijah to repair the old altar on Mt. Carmel before he would send down fire, and the same is true in every age. Before God will send down fire, His altars of truth and righteousness need to be repaired. Revivalist preacher Vance Havner once wrote, *Here is our task, to repair these broken altars, and all our pious dodges and clever substitutes to avoid repentance will never avail. Stained glass windows and robed choirs and anthems and banquets and dramas and eloquence in the pulpit and eloquence in the pew have never fooled God. He demands truth in the inward parts, and heaven will keep silent and no fire will ever fall until we approach Him with rebuilt altars in the name of the Lord.*[44]

As we will see in the next few days, many altars needed to be repaired in the 1790s before God sent His awakening fires. The rationalism, deism, and fanatical pursuit of "liberty" promoted by Thomas Paine and the French Revolution dismantled many an altar from which, at one time, God's truth and righteousness had been taught. From the soldiers who came home from the war doubting the reliability of God's word, thanks to their French allies, to the young people who were being indoctrinated on college campuses, and to the many pulpits in churches where "new doctrines" were being taught, the altars of truth and righteousness were being dismantled stone by stone.

Just as in the days of Elijah, God was preserving a faithful remnant who did not bow down or kiss Baal. They longed to see the day when old altars were rebuilt and fire from heaven fell upon God's people. Oh, how they longed to hear from their neighbors and their own prodigal children, *The Lord—He is God! The Lord—He is God!* Oh, how they prayed to see churches filled to capacity with people singing the praises of the one and only Lord and Savior of the world!

These faithful were encouraged by modern day Elijahs and Elishas who faithfully preached and defended the truth of God's word, even when it was not popular to do so. They led by example, fervently praying when many were giving up hope. These tireless servants of the Lord did not cave in to the temptation to fill their emptying pews with words designed merely to "tickle ears" and "keep everyone happy." No, they kept on preaching and teaching the whole counsel of God's word with even greater passion. They took to heart both God's promises and His warnings to the churches.

In the next several days, we will meet a few of these faithful leaders and learn how God used them to rebuild His altars, often serving in communities and alongside churches not unlike those described in the book of Revelation.

As we study five of the seven churches described in the book of Revelation and relate them to churches and individuals living in the 1790s, ask the Lord to search your own heart. It is the height of arrogance and hypocrisy to pray fervently for revival in the Church and nation when revival needs first to take place in our own hearts and lives. When you and I become submissive to the Lordship of Christ—there will be fervent prayer!

Before God sends down fire . . . His altars of truth and righteousness need to be repaired.

Reflect upon these thoughts and pray.

Do you know any spiritual leaders in our society today or in your church who remind you of Elijah? What "Elijah" type qualities do they possess? Pray that the Lord will encourage these modern day prophets, and that God will raise up many more like them.

(Daily reading: I Kings 18:16-30)

Day 14

Charity for All

To the angel of the church in Ephesus write...
You have forsaken your first love.
(Rev. 2:1)

We don't know for sure why John's vision begins here at Ephesus. Perhaps this was the first church on a postal route. More than likely, it was located in the foremost city of Asia Minor and the home of the most influential church in that part of the world. In fact, Ephesus became the epicenter of evangelistic work throughout Asia Minor according to Acts 19:10. It was the first and oldest church among the seven churches.

Now I want you to imagine being a Christian living in Ephesus at the time of this letter. Imagine how difficult it must have been to raise a Christian family and maintain your Christian walk with the Lord here in this city. Let's begin by imagining your little eight-year-old son coming home from playing with other children in the neighborhood and wearing some kind of amulet or necklace with a purple bag tied to the end of it. You question your son, and he runs away from you until you finally confront him with a question, asking him what is inside the purple bag. He reluctantly takes out a piece of lime wood with the following message etched on it: *Hekate, Artemis, Kronos, and Aphrodite guard me from Daimon of the air, on the earth and from every angel and ghostly visitation.*[45] He sheepishly tells you that all of the young people are wearing them for protection these days.

Now go on and imagine that your 18-year-old son has started an apprenticeship at a local silversmith shop. Things were going well until the boss got this huge order to construct Artemis idols for the many tourists who travel to Ephesus each year to honor this fertility goddess. Your son has an important decision to make. He can either quit his hard-to-come-by apprenticeship or continue making idols.

The father of this imaginary family works in the docks. Ephesus has an enormous port, and every night he walks home down a huge street, thirty-five feet wide, lined with columns. Standing by each column is temptation, women willing to sell themselves for trinkets to any lonely traveler or dockworker. Every day he walks home with hundreds of women throwing themselves at his feet.

Of course, we cannot forget the wife and mother of this family. She desires some culture, and Ephesus is full of it. Ephesus' greatest prize was the large theatre, which sat on a slope overlooking the harbor. It seated 25,000 people. Now imagine our housewife going to a drama. Most of the early dramas were Greek tragedies. She looks forward to an afternoon of getting away with her friends, but before the play begins, the orchestra comes out with an animal, and they kill it on an altar as a way to honor the gods and to honor the emperor. She feels like walking out, but walking out would be a sign of treason to the emperor and to the empire.

This early Christian family was living in a world totally antithetical and hostile to their faith. They needed their church fellowship to stay faithful and to keep growing in the truth. Their church placed a heavy emphasis on the letters of the apostles. Their children knew right from wrong, and they all had a clear grasp of how to live the Christian Faith. In fact, their understanding of the Christian Faith and their persistence to stay faithful to apostolic truth enabled them to spot a false teacher a mile away. The Lord Jesus even praised them for not getting caught up with the Nicolaitan sect, which was running through other churches like wildfire. Not in Ephesus!

What is not to like about this faithful old church? From the surface, this church looks like a model for other churches to emulate. While their love and devotion to Christ may have existed, their love for a lost world, and possibly for each other, was but a glimmer of its past brightness. It all adds up, doesn't it—a culture and city that hates you and your standards . . . a plethora of false teachers lurking everywhere you go . . . demonic influences saturating every aspect of society. Yes, it all adds up to conditions that are ripe for creating a "bunker" Christianity. The fear of the culture, felt by the faithful of Ephesus, raised the bar of their suspicion and defensiveness to the point that they stopped demonstrating the love of Christ to a city in desperate need of it. Their faith had developed into a form of legalism, which set such a high standard for people to follow that it lacked grace and Christian love for others who were struggling in their faith.

Ultimately, legalism of this kind is nothing more than a badge of pride for those who believe that they have "mastered" all Christian truth and are able to rise above their culture. The next step in such lives is to wait patiently for Jesus to take them home. Nothing else matters! *Leave the Ephesian people to perish in their idolatry, and they will leave us alone to worship Jesus!*

The American churches of the 1790s had their share of exclusivity, which prevented parts of the Church from fervently praying for the next awakening. There were old animosities and suspicions from the days of the war. Some had a raging hatred of the Indians and despised the notion of Indian missions. There were still others in the churches who developed a theology of slavery, which enabled them, in "good conscience," to treat their African slaves as sub-human.

In every age, there are churches and individual Christians who build up protective walls to keep society out and to keep the Church in. Some of these walls are poor excuses, raised out of needless fear. Others are walls built from the mortar of pride and legalism. Still other insulated walls are built around people and institutions by insecure and/or manipulative spiritual leaders.

Before churches will experience God's power in new and fresh ways, they need to hear what the Spirit says concerning their fellowship and its love for Christ and for each other. Then, they must repent, as the Spirit convicts.

Reflect upon these thoughts pray.

Is there any animosity or prejudice toward anyone in your heart? Ask the Lord to show you if there is any resentment or hatred toward someone, and if there is, confess it before Him. Submit yourself to the Lord of the Church, as He places you on a path of reconciliation.

(Daily reading: Revelation 2:1-7)

Day 15

Father Mills

Samuel John Mills was born in Kent, Connecticut, in 1743. Samuel was raised on a farm by Christian parents who taught all of their five children the basics of the Christian Faith and the necessity of prayer. Walking with a friend by the house where he was raised, Samuel Mills said, *Yonder, did my father direct my little brother to go night and morning, and call upon God; and yonder, behind that other object did he charge me to go and perform the same service.*[46]

Mills attended Yale College and graduated in 1764 at the age of twenty-one. For the next two years, he was tutored for ministry by Rev. Joel Bordwell, and he became a candidate for ministry in 1767. He received a call from the Torrington Congregational Church in 1769, and served as their pastor for over fifty years, outliving all of his Yale classmates. He also outlived his wife, Esther, who passed away in 1809. Samuel and Esther had seven children.

This remarkable man began his ministry in Torrington while the northern part of the area was being cleared and settled for farms. Times were difficult for these pioneers and even more difficult for the pastor whom they supported. The first five years were challenging, but nothing like the trials that followed as the colonies went to war against Great Britain. The seven long years of war were fearful times

> *A black man came to his back door on an errand and Mr. Mills said to him, "Why did you come to the back door? When you come to my house, come to the front door, for we shall all go into heaven by one door.*
>
> *-A neighbor of Mr. Mills*

of deprivation and personal loss to his congregation. Rev. Mills, as a tenderhearted pastor, was up to the challenge. He loved his flock and demonstrated sacrificial mercy to the poor and suffering and gracious hospitality to anyone who came to visit. One day a poor woman came to the door while Esther Mills was setting the dinner table. She had just put out a loaf of bread and had left the room. Samuel took the loaf, handed it to the poor woman, and told her to cover it with her apron and carry it home. When Mrs. Mills came back into the room soon after, she asked what had become of the loaf of bread; Samuel replied, Madame, are you sure you put any bread on the table?[47] This man loved people because he loved his Lord. He was, as Luther Hart preached at the funeral for Samuel Mills, eminently a man of prayer.[48]

The most striking aspect of this man was his evangelistic zeal. He would often melt to tears while preaching or speaking about evangelical subjects. "Father Mills," as he was fondly called by many people in the Litchfield, Connecticut, area, had a glowing passion for evangelism. His life's theme and vision was, "Souls and Salvation." It was said of him:

> If in the impression he made on others there was one thing more prominent than another, it was his very great anxiety, and eagerness to lead men from the danger of a sinful life to safety under the light of the gospel, and so fully was this true that the unconverted seemed almost anxious to help him and willing to become the subjects of saving grace, so as to relieve the concern which he felt in their behalf and to cause him to rejoice.[49]

This evangelistic zeal brought growth and renewal to the Torrington area as eight different revivals were said to have blessed Father Mill's pastorate in his fifty years of ministry. The greatest of revivals undoubtedly happened during the 1790s after one of the most difficult times, both in the Torrington Church and in the young nation.

It was said that these times disheartened Father Mills more than the seven years of war. From 1784 to 1799, the dark period of infidelity cast its shadow over Torrington. As the call for liberty and freedom from all oppression and oppressive institutions sounded in France, its reverberations were felt across the ocean in the United States. Infatuated with France, Americans were also looking to free themselves from the oppression of a greedy bourgeois class and the morally stifling ecclesiastical monopolies of New England. In 1784, the state constitution of Connecticut changed concerning the support of gospel ministry. This change liberated citizens from having to support religious societies. Many able and influential members withdrew their support and their allegiance from the Torrington church. Others withdrew from Father Mills and the Torrington church because of theological issues. Samuel Mills was a staunch Calvinist who taught the "doctrines of grace," which included the sovereignty of God. On one occasion, while Samuel Mills was preaching on this subject, a prominent man stood up in the congregation and exclaimed, *Mr. Mills, you make machines of us all, you do!*, and stormed out of the church in the midst of the service.

Despite the objections voiced by some who found his theology offensive, Samuel Mills faithfully preached God's word and courageously preached the doctrine of God's sovereignty. One of his biographers wrote, *It did not matter to him how angry men became under such preaching, for he charged them with being angry with God; not with the interpretations the minister gave but with God, and it was a very strong evidence of their very great hardness of heart and the greater need that they should be humbled. . .*[50]

This faithful pastor continued to preach the truth, pray earnestly, and as a "father" to many of the neighboring clergy, he encouraged them to do the same. In the dark days of infidelity, when morals were at an all-time low and historic orthodox views of the Bible, Christ, and the way of salvation were despised, Father Mills held his ground and did not waver. As we will see later on, his heart for missions and his respect for all people, regardless of color, had a great impact upon the next generation of spiritual leaders.

Reflect upon these thoughts and pray.

What message did the life and ministry of Father Mills communicate to both the community and to his congregation?

Lord, I pray for the pastors and leaders of churches across the country. Help them to stand firmly planted upon your word. Bring a spiritual renewal among all church leaders and lead them to come together, even across denominational lines, to pray fervently for each other and for their churches. Amen.

(Daily reading: Acts 20:25-38)

Day 16

Relevance Gone Amok

To the angel of the church in Pergamum write...
You have people there who hold to the teaching of Balaam ...
Likewise you also have those who hold to the teachings of the Nicolaitans.
(Rev.2:12,14)

Pergamum was the capital city of Asia Minor. The Lord called it the "seat of Satan." There is some debate why the Lord gave it this dubious distinction. Pergamum was built on a huge hill; in fact, you could see the Mediterranean Ocean from the peak of the hill, some 15 miles away. On the top of this huge hill stood a temple dedicated to the Greek god Zeus. The temple extended out from the hill upon a terrace that looked like a throne when you viewed the temple from down below. Could this be the reason why the Lord called it the seat or throne of Satan?

There is another possible reason why Christ called this city the seat of Satan. It was the regional center for the worship of the emperor. The emperor was regarded to be the very incarnation of the spirit of Rome; therefore, he believed that he deserved to be worshipped. Anyone who refused to confess, "Caesar is Lord," was considered to be not only an "atheist," but also a traitor to the empire.

Christ's letter to this church begins on a very positive note. The Christians here refused to say, "Caesar is Lord." One such man, Antipas, died a martyr's death because he refused to confess it. He stood up against the seat of Satan by confessing, "Jesus is Lord!"

Nevertheless, the Lord of the Church was not pleased with His church in Pergamum. They had a few people in the church who held to the teachings of Balaam and of the Nicolaitans. Who were these people and what did they teach?

If you go back to the Old Testament, to Numbers, chapter 25, you can read about Balaam. He was the prophet who beat his donkey until the donkey stopped and started to talk back to him. Balaam was a sort of "prophet for hire," or, if you prefer, a "prophet for profit." He was hired by the Moabite king Balak to curse the Israelites. When that didn't happen, Balaam suggested a different approach—women. If the Israelite men could be seduced sexually, they could also be seduced to worship idols, threatening their relationship with the Lord.

There were people within the church of Pergamum who became enamored with the teachings of the Nicolaitans—a sect of Christianity founded on the principle that since Christians have liberty and freedom in Christ, they can do or be engaged in any immoral or pagan practice, because a Christian is saved by grace. The "Balaamites" were people who missed their old social gatherings and entertainment venues, which were often centered on the worship of idols. The teachings of the Nicolaitans opened the door for these people to return to their old ways of life, causing no offense to their old friends. They could live, work and play in Pergamum without standing out or creating suspicion about their contrary views of emperor worship. They could even make Christianity a relevant and appealing option for people looking for some new spiritual experience. They wanted to mainstream Christianity. It was Ephesus in reverse and relevance gone amok!

Is it any wonder then why the Lord of the Church addressed the Pergamum Christians with such forceful words! The Lord described Himself as the One with a double-edged sword. The people in Pergamum knew all about the sword. As the capital of the Asian province, they had a proconsul who was given the right of the sword. He and he alone had the right to execute a person on the spot. Jesus told the Pergamum Church that no matter what kind of pressure or persecution they might face in the city because of their faith, He was ultimately the One who wielded the double-edged sword. Jesus is the ultimate judge.

As I reflect upon Christ's warning to them, I wonder what it's like to have the Lord of the Church fight against one of His own. It is an indication of how serious Christ took the threat of compromise with the gods of this world. Thank the Lord for today's prophets who speak His word of conviction to hearts that have become too infatuated with the world.

Reflect upon these thoughts and pray.

Have you ever experienced the sharp sword of God's word upon your heart? If so, what did the Lord convict you of and how did you respond to Him? Is there such a thing as making Christianity too "relevant" for the world?

Lord, search my heart today with your very sharp sword. Show me areas of weakness, hypocrisy, and even hidden sins lodged deep within my heart. Please lead me to a renewed relationship with You. Amen.

(Daily reading: Revelation 2:12-17)

Day 17

Chauncey's Pudding

Charles Chauncey (1705-1787) was the pastor of Boston's First Church. While serving as junior pastor under the powerful ministry of Thomas Foxcroft, Chauncey became irritated when George Whitefield was invited by Foxcroft to preach. Afterwards, he wrote an anyomous letter attacking Whitefield, but it wasn't until James Davenport's divisive ministry as a revivalist preacher that Chauncey began to grow in popularity and persuasion among New England's Congregational leaders. Chauncey had compiled a 424-page diatribe that highlighted abuses, divisions, and ecstatic spiritual experiences stemming from the Great Awakening. Admittedly, there were some abuses during the First Great Awakening, but Chauncey didn't like the direction in which the Church was moving, as the Spirit was moving in ways Chauncey couldn't control.

At the center of it all was Chauncey's fear of the church becoming anti-intellectual and, therefore, unappealing to the sophisticated classes of people who lived in Boston and to the eyes of the world. This was a period of growing scientific discoveries and rational skepticism of all traditions and institutions—even within the Church.

Chauncey's solution was what he privately called, *the pudding*, and it detailed a new discovery he had made. Chauncey claimed to have stumbled upon an earth-shattering truth that had been hidden from the Church. His contentions were that the New Testament had been misread for over two thousand years, and that through this new style of biblical interpretation that he had discovered, he had received a new understanding of the Bible for this *singularly regenerate moment in religious history.*[51] Chauncey's "discovery" was put in writing in 1750, but only a few like-minded clergy were made privy to his new understanding of Christianity. He called it the pudding, as a code name when referring to his discoveries, because he was afraid the public wasn't ready for his ideas to be revealed in 1750. The secret pudding would only be shared with "learned clergy" who were open to his new interpretation of Scripture. Eventually, Chauncey's young ministerial collegues pushed him to publish an anonymous pamplett in 1782 entitled, *Salvation for all Men, Illustrated and Vindicated as a Scripture Doctrine.* The pudding was finally dished out of its bowl.

What was this *pudding?* Chauncey's *pudding* was based upon the premise that hell was not necessarily an eternal judgement. Using Taylor's interpretation of the Greek word αἰώνος used to describe duration, Chauncey argued that it could also be translated, a very long and finite time period, over against its traditonal and historical meaning of "forever." With this new discovery, he was able to formulate a view of Christianity that would appeal to almost everyone and still be, in his own mind, true to his New England theological tradition.[52] He became the father of what is known as "Universalism."

Chauncey's attempt to make the Church relevant and mainstream in the eighteenth century added to the spiritual and moral decline of the young country in the 1790s. Sermons became formal and passionless. The evangelical call to save the perishing was silenced in these churches, because the belief that God is too loving to send anyone to hell—at least for a long period of time—began to permeate the Church's thinking. Institutions like Harvard spawned classes of future leaders with little or no commitment to biblical truth. Chauncey was one of many who tore down the altars of the Lord.

Reflect upon these thoughts and pray.

Do you see examples today of churches or church leaders who are compromising the historic and orthodox teachings of the Bible in order to reach younger generations? Do you see examples of this in your own church? Commit these churches and church leaders to prayer. Ask the Lord to change their thinking and lead them to rebuild the broken down altars.

(Daily reading: Jude 8:17-23)

Day 18

Jezebel Returns

To the angel of the church in Thyatira write. . .
Nevertheless, I have this against you:
You tolerate that woman Jezebel, who calls herself a prophetess.
(Rev. 2:18, 20)

For all the progess made in the church of Thyatira, there was an enemy who was destroying this fellowship from within. The Lord of the Church described this enemy with a fitting name—Jezebel. A thousand years before the existance of the Thyatira Church, Jezebel, the wife of king Ahab, had imported her demonic influence into the very fabric of Israeli life. She had such a beguiling influence over her husband that she was able to introduce every kind of foul occultic practice imaginable into the culture of Israel. Jezebel brought decay to Israel from within. That is exactly what this new prophetess was doing in Thyatira.

This city was known for its trade guilds. These early forms of the Masonic Lodge had their own trade secrets in a variety of industries such as leather making, pottery, and especially the fabric industry (see Acts 16:14). These guild "meetings" also included feasts where sacrifces of meat were offered to idols, and partipants were treated to all the wine and women they wanted. If you were in a trade, you had to be a member of a guild, and you had to be an active particpant in the guild. Christians living in Thyatira inevitably suffered loss of buisness and income by refusing to participate in some or all of the guild activities. That is, until Jezebel showed up.

We don't know who she was, but we do know that she was responsible for giving Christians permission to practice all the vile things associated with the guilds. She came to church with what she said was the Word of the Lord, and the people of Thyatira allowed her to lead them. Even after she was warned not to teach, presumably by John or some other apostle, she continued to sanction the believers' full participation in the guilds.

Notice the warning against this woman. The Lord of the Church was going to cast both her and those flirting with her onto a bed of suffering. Paul told the Christians in Corinth something similar. In I Corinthians 11:30, he gave the reason why many in their fellowship were weak and sick: They were eating the Lord's Supper in an unworthy manner. Reading on in I Corinthians, Paul tells us that some were living in open rebellion, even applauding the sexual deviance of one of its members. The Lord sent sickness and even death to some as a form of discipline. The same warning was being issued here for those who tolerated this prophetess in their fellowship.

The warning became even more threatening for those who were her disciples, children (Rev. 2, vs. 23). These were people who were so enamored by this false prophetess that there seemed to be no hope for them. Their judgment was imminent death—perhaps as a warning to all the other churches in Asia Minor that the Lord of the Church would not tolerate another Jezebel.

We should not be surprised by this teaching as we think back through Church history. Many have died as a result of following the teachings of Jezebel-like prophets. Hundreds of people died following Rev. Jim Jones to his "utopian" world in Guyana. Or consider the deaths of many in Waco, Texas, under the leadership of David Koresh and the Branch Davidians. They, too, followed Koresh as "father" and were manipulated by the twisted teachings of Koresh's brand of Christianity. Sadly, despite pleas from family and friends to leave these cultic leaders, their pleas fell upon deaf ears and hardened hearts.

As I study the condition of the Thyatira Church, I see a discernment problem within the membership of that fellowship. Where were the Christians with the spiritual gift of discernment? The Lord of the Church is described as the One with blazing eyes who is able to discern the hearts of men. Why didn't anyone pray for wisdom from the One with blazing eyes? Where were the "Berean" type of Christians who would examine the Scriptures every day to see if what (Jezebel) said was true and then respond accordingly? Where was the leadership of this church? If she had been warned by the apostles not to teach, why did they let her continue?

Perhaps the fear and anxiety of being guild outcastes caused the people of Tyatira to give Jezebel the green light to continue teaching. A message encouraging one to take the path of least resistance is always popular until it is too late, and the followers realize that it leads to their destruction.

In the latter part of the 18th century, the nation of France had its own Jezebels. They had names like Voltaire and Rousseau and many others, including some American writers such as Thomas Paine and Ethan Allen. These writers assailed the historicity of the Bible, and the person and work of Christ, in order to free people from the superstitions and tyrany of the Church. Salvation, they all wrote, comes from within man's own power and intellect. France had few, if any, prophets who could or would take these men to task. The result was a bloody revolution and an even bloodier dictatorship.

The United States was being infected by the same Jezebels in the 1790s. This poison had infected pastors, college students, and many of the day's political leaders. America needed a prophet who could go head-to-head with Jezebel's prophets, rebuilding the very foundations of the Lord's altars. But was there such a prophet living in the United States during this time?

Reflect upon these thoughts and pray.

Ask the One with blazing eyes to search your mind and heart. Ask Him to show you areas of spiritual weakness in your own life. Ask Him also to show you times, if any, where you compromised your leadership at home, work, or even at church in order to take the path of least resistance. Confess these areas of weakness and compromise to the Lord of the Church. Turn from them and ask for and receive His forgiveness.

(Daily reading: Revelation 2:18-29)

Day 19

Dr. Dwight and the Kids

As the new President of Yale College in 1795, one of the many hats Timothy Dwight wore was that of pastor of the college church. During that first wintery season, as the new president of Yale, he walked into the chapel to preach on a Sunday morning and found only one student out of 110 in attendance.[53] Many in the very first class that Dwight taught as president not only claimed their skepticism of Christianity, they also took on the names of their favorite French philosophers as they greeted one another. Can you imagine Timothy Dwight listening to one student address another by the name of "Mr. Voltaire" and the other returning the greeting, "Mr. Rousseau"?[54] That was the spiritual landscape Dwight found at Yale College when he became president of his alma mater.

Timothy Dwight was born into a home and lineage of spiritual leaders, the most famous being his grandfather, Jonathon Edwards. Timothy was born in 1752, and was raised in the same Congregational church in Northampton, Massachusetts, where his grandfather had been fired just two years prior to Timothy's birth.[55] Dwight's father was a Yale graduate (1744) and a businessman, with impressive land holdings around the Northampton area. According to Timothy's brother Sereno, *He was a man of sound understanding, of fervent piety, and of great purity of life.*[56]

Timothy's mother married young and became a mother at the age of eighteen. She possessed a sharp intellect and was well-schooled, thanks, in part, to the many scholars who had visited and stayed in the Edwards' home as she was growing up. Mary was a firm believer in preparing children to learn as soon as possible, rejecting the notion that small children were too young to be educated. Consequently, young Timothy was able to read the entire Bible at the age of four and began studying Latin at the age of six. Both parents, through example and teaching, impressed upon young Timothy the doctrine of grace and how to live a moral and charitable life.

At the young age of thirteen, Timothy enrolled at Yale College. His first two years of college life were wasted because of faculty upheaval, lax discipline, personal sickness, and temptations, as he was thrown into a world of older and more "worldly" teenagers who loved to gamble. While Timothy never played for money, he did fall prey to the addictive allurement of gambling, and it became a habit that consumed his time and talents. Through the kind and insightful care and counsel of his tutor, Stephen Mix Mitchell, Timothy was encouraged to take his studies more seriously. Mitchell saw with pain the potential that was going to waste and helped the young teen become the kind of student and future scholar that the Lord had intended him to become. Dwight covenanted to become more serious and productive. By his third year at Yale, Dwight was reading fourteen hours a day. He continued to do so until his eyes were weakened and permanently damaged after an attack of smallpox. This weakness and pain of the eyes plagued Dwight for the rest of his life. Timothy also pursued his interest in poetry[57] and music, writing hymns and collecting sacred music, as he became a serious college student.

Dwight graduated from Yale in the year 1769, at the age of seventeen. He taught school in New Haven for two years and then received an appointment to become a tutor at Yale College. It was during this time as a tutor that Dwight became serious about his Christian Faith and made a profession of his faith in the college church.[58] This was also a time of soul-searching as he considered whether he should go on and study law or enter the ministry. The Lord led him to ministry, and in 1777, he was licensed to preach. In the same year, he married his wife,

Mary Woolsey, from Long Island.

As war broke out against England, the classes at Yale were suspended. In 1777, Dwight became a military chaplain, serving under the command of General Putnum, until word reached him that his father had died,[59] and he was needed back home. Dwight moved his family back to Northampton to provide for his widowed mother and her thirteen children, ten of whom were under the age of twenty-one. For five years, Dwight farmed and provided for his own family and that of his mother and siblings. Timothy, ever productive, kept busy preaching in area churches, as he started his own school. The sacrifice and commitment that he made to his mother and family, as he postponed his own plans, speaks volumes about the man God used to become a modern day Elijah. In fact, his integrity and sacrifice caught the attention of many residents in Northampton. They chose him to represent them in the Massachusetts legislature in 1781. He once again proved himself exceptional, and there was a growing movement to recruit him to serve in the new Constitutional Congress, making politics his life profession. Dwight flatly rejected their prestigious offers, and in 1783, he became the pastor of the Greenfield Congregational Church.

Education of the future generation was always a passion of Timothy Dwight, and at Greenfield, he once again started a school. The Greenfield Academy grew in prominence within the state of Connecticut and throughout the colonies. Dwight worked tirelessly as he pastored the church, spending an average of six hours daily teaching and administrating the school, even raising funds to support it. He also opened up his own home to board twenty to twenty-five students. His academy was one of the first in New England to enroll girls. In the twelve years that he was at Greenfield, he instructed over 1,000 students. He was well loved and greatly respected by both his parishioners and his students.

The twelve years Dwight spent at Greenfield, and his earlier teaching and administrative roles at Yale and in Northampton, helped Dwight shape his educational principles and embolden his vision to make higher education accessible and culturally transformative. He wanted to help students make independent and responsible decisions. He broke with the old standards of education that were based on rigid law enforcement, and instead pursued a course that placed the responsibility for a misdemeanor on the perpetrator, rather than on the parents. Dwight sought to make the child responsible for his own behavior by appeals to the conscience, by the use of counseling, and, if all else failed, expulsion.[60]

His reputation and his proven success in education made the Greenfield Academy an attractive alternative to some of the better known schools and colleges. In fact, Dwight's success as an educator was so well known that his school rivaled Yale as a place of learning for Connecticut youth (much to the discomfort of Ezra Stiles).[61] It was at Greenfield where the Lord began to use this eighteenth-century Elijah. In 1788, Dwight published a satirical poem entitled, *The Triumph of Infidelity,* which was aimed at exposing the dangers of the universalism of Charles Chauncey.[62] In 1794, he published a message he had delivered a year earlier entitled, *Discourse on the Genuineness and Authenticity of the New Testament*; this publication had a huge impact upon the churches in Connecticut, as it was used as a well-reasoned defense against biblical skepticism.

Dwight's Eighteenth Century Mt. Carmel

The Lord found him faithful in Greenfield, and then he "promoted" him to a place of historic and national influence. Dwight took on the prophets of Baal in his own version of Mt. Carmel. His gifted intellect, his educational experiences, and his personal gravitas were the tools God used to take on the prophets of Baal at Yale, and even beyond!

As Dwight rebuilt the altars of the historic Christian Faith at Yale, he didn't repeat the same mistakes the previous administration had made by suppressing the issues of skepticism and the students' infatuation with the French philosophers. Rather, Dwight challenged the *prophets of Baal* to a debate. One of the subjects that the senior class had chosen for their senior debates was the topic, *Are the Scriptures of the Old and New Testaments the Word of God?* The students never imagined that they would be permitted to debate such a topic at Yale. Yet that was precisely the topic Dwight chose. As the seniors gladly and arrogantly collected every fact and prepared every argument against the Bible being God's word, they were not surprised to find that their only opponent was Dr. Dwight.

Like the priests of Baal on Mt. Carmel, they presented their arguments as champions of infidelity. When everyone had fully stated his case, it was Dwight's turn to speak. It was a landslide victory for Dwight, the historic Christian Faith, and most importantly, for the glory of God. Dwight made short work of all of their arguments, proving their statements of fact to be either wrong or irrelevant. He then presented his case with such positive proofs and animated eloquence that even the stoutest infidel in the class was left dumbfounded. The debate sent ripples of shock throughout Yale. Dwight's biographer, Charles Cunningham, wrote, *Almost before the campaign had opened, this decisive victory at the outset started the rout of infidelity.*[63]

This small victory was but the opening salvo for what would become a major bombardment, as Dwight went on to preach for six months on the subject of "Divine Revelation." In fact, Dwight went on to preach every day at the forenoon chapel services with a series of sermons lasting four years, and then he repeated the sermons to every new freshman class. These sermons provided the stones and mortar to rebuild broken-down altars at Yale and in churches throughout the United States.

Reflect upon these thoughts and pray.

Can you think of any pastors, scholars, or church leaders who are actively engaging modern day anti-Christian philosophies or are actively defending the historic Christian Faith from the enemies within the Church? Pray for them and their apologetic ministries. Pray that the Lord will raise up modern day Timothy Dwights, who have the intelligence and fortitude to stand up to modern day critics of God's word and who will rebuild the broken altars of truth among college students.

(Daily reading: Ezra 8:1-8)

Day 20

A Thief in the Night

To the angel of the church in Sardis write...
Wake up! Strengthen what remains and is about to die...
(Rev. 3:1, 2)

I remember talking with my next door neighbor a few years ago after he returned from his yearly physical. Mike was around 75-years old and was overweight. When I asked him about his check-up, he repeated the words the doctor had just told him. *Mike,* the doctor said, *I judge it will take at least ten strong men. Mike asked him, What are you talking about? Ten strong men for what? The doctor grimly responded, Ten strong men to carry out your casket unless you get into shape by losing some weight.* In Revelation 3, the Lord of the Church has some equally strong warnings for the church of Sardis.

The church of Sardis needed a wakeup call too. Sardis was a church living off its past reputation of being spiritually alive and active. However, in the present, they were lethargic and spiritually asleep, while they left the world around them and the members within their own fellowship unguarded. It seems almost ironic that Christ would call this church to wake up and be on guard. Years earlier, the city had been under siege by the Persian army who were waiting for the right opportunity to make their way into the impregnable city of Sardis. Eventually they found a hidden passage in the rocks. As they made their way into the city, they found that the battle placements were left unguarded. *The citizens of Sardis had smugly thought that their city was safe: No one has ever been able to penetrate our city*—so they thought.

What had happened centuries earlier to the city of Sardis was repeating itself spiritually in the church of Sardis. This time, the thief in the night would not be the Persians, but the Lord himself, coming in judgment.

How did this church become so spiritually sluggish? The answer is in Chapter 3, verse 4, of Revelation, *Yet you have a few people in Sardis who have not soiled their clothes.* A majority of the Christians in Sardis had become too cozy with the world. Whenever you find a lethargic Christian, more than likely, that person is too heavily involved with the things of the world to be concerned with the heavenly things of the Kingdom of God. The Apostle Paul wrote to the young Pastor Timothy, *No one serving as a soldier gets involved with civilian affairs——he wants to please his commanding officer.* (II Timothy 2:4). The author of Hebrews encourages Christians to . . . *throw off everything that hinders and the sin that so easily entangles, and let us run the race with perseverance* (Hebrews 12:1).

The Bible repeatedly warns, through example and teaching, of the dangers of being too involved with the things of this world, which will entangle us and divert our attention away from our Commander and Chief and the Christian race we are called to run. When we become *unequally yoked* with people, institutions, or even movements in culture that are not Kingdom-based, our hearts soon un-friend King Jesus. When this begins to happen, we no longer have time to worship or spend time alone with the Lord. We find that our time and all our other resources are slowly being diverted into worldly accounts, instead of heavenly ones. Eventually, we find ourselves not ready to meet the Lord when He comes as a thief in the night.

Reflect upon these thoughts and pray.

Have you been growing in your faith and serving the Lord with the same passion and perseverance as you had when you first became a Christian? If not, ask the Lord to show you your heart. Ask Him to show you the "soiled" parts of your life and confess them before Him, so that you may be ready whenever Christ returns.

(Daily reading: Revelation 3:1-6)

Day 21

Adoniram's Fearful Night

When we left Adoniram Judson (Day 6), he had just told his parents about his skepticism concerning the Bible and the entire Christian Faith. His father's defense contained more smoke than fire, and his mother cried and prayed. When Adoniram left his parents, he prided himself in the fact that his father's arguments were no match for the skepticism he had developed in his own mind. Since before he entered college, Adoniram had tried to hinder the work of the Holy Spirit. After his near fatal illness he considered his life's purpose and confessed, that religion seemed so entirely opposed to all his ambitious plans that he was afraid to look into his heart, lest he should discover what he did not like to confess, even to himself— that he did not want to become a Christian.[64]

As a college student, he was already at work trying to dismantle the altar of truth established within him by Christian parents and the Christian community. His dismantling of those altars became even easier when he "yoked" himself with Jacob Eames. The two of them constructed "new altars" to replace the old, so that their consciences could be eased and ambitious plans pursued for their own glory. Nonetheless, his mother and, presumably, his father, kept praying for him.

When Adoniram walked away from his parents to begin looking for adventure in New York City, he knew he was on the verge of living a life that, in his heart, he truly despised. He left for New York believing that he was not in any real danger. He told himself that he was merely going to see both the dark and the bright sides of the world, and that he had too much self-respect to do anything immoral or mean.

After seeing what he wanted of New York City, he decided to go westward, so he returned to Sheffield to obtain a new horse from his uncle's stables. The Rev. Ephraim Judson was not home to help him, but a godly young Christian man helped him find a suitable steed for the trip. The young man was a very sincere Christian, and both his conversation and his loving example made a deep impression upon Adoniram.

As he began his trip westward, Adoniram stopped at a country inn for the night. The following describes what he experienced during that night.

> The landlord mentioned, as he lighted him to his room, that he had been obliged to place him next door to a young man who was exceedingly ill, probably in a dying state; but he hoped that it would occasion him no uneasiness. Judson assured him that, beyond pity for the poor sick man, he should have no feeling whatever, and that now, having heard of the circumstance, his pity would now of course be increased by the nearness of the object. But it was, nevertheless, a very restless night. Sounds came from the sick-chamber—sometimes the movements of the watchers, sometimes the groans of the sufferer; but it was not these which disturbed him. He thought of what the landlord had said—the stranger was probably in a dying state; and was he prepared? Alone, and in the dead of night, he felt a blush of shame steal over him at the question, for it proved the shallowness of his philosophy. What would his late companions say to his weakness? The clear-minded, intellectual, witty Eames, what would he say to such consummate boyishness? But still his thoughts would revert to the sick man. Was he a Christian, calm and strong in the hope of a glorious immortality, or was he shuddering upon the brink of a dark, unknown future? Perhaps he was

> a 'freethinker,' educated by Christian parents, and prayed over by a Christian mother. The landlord had described him as a young man; and in imagination he was forced to place himself upon the dying bed, though he strove with all his might against it. At last morning came, and the bright flood of light which it poured into his chamber dispelled all his 'superstitious illusions.' As soon as he had risen, he went in search of the landlord, and inquired for his fellow-lodger. "He is dead," was the reply. "Dead!" "Yes, he is gone, poor fellow! The doctor said he would probably not survive the night." "Do you know who he was?" "O, yes; it was a young man from Providence College—a very fine fellow; his name was Eames." Judson was completely stunned. After hours had passed, he knew not how, he attempted to pursue his journey. But one single thought occupied his mind, and the words, "Dead! Lost! Lost!" were continually ringing in his ears. He knew the religion of the Bible to be true; he felt its truth; and he was in despair. In this state of mind, he resolved to abandon his scheme of travelling, and at once turned his horse's head toward Plymouth.[65]

The thief in the night came for Jacob Eames and Adoniram Judson woke up. On September 22, 1808, Adoniram entered the new and orthodox theological seminary at Andover. Here, even though he was not a Christian, nor was he preparing to become a candidate for the ministry, the Lord started to rebuild his torn down altars and give him a hunger to know the truth. Within four months of rebuilding that altar, Adoniram Judson had committed his life to Christ and had consecrated his future to the Lord for ministry.

Reflect upon these thoughts and pray.

Do you have family or friends who are spiritually asleep and who are unprepared to meet the Lord if they should die today? If you find yourself apathetic to their plight, imagine, just as Adoniram did, that you were the person dying in the other room—dying without the Savior.

Lord, today I bring before You the names of people who I fear are spiritually lost and need You as their Savior and Lord. Begin a good work in their hearts and lead them to the cross. Amen.

(Daily reading: Hebrew 10:19-39)

Day 22

Luke Warm and Lovin' It

To the angel of the church in Laodicea write . . .
I know your deeds, that you are neither cold nor hot.
I wish you were either one or the other!
(Rev. 3:14, 15)

Our final "unhealthy" church is Laodicea. Here was a rich and smug church. They had wealth in this life and assurance of salvation for the world to come. We don't read of any persecution against this church, even though we know that there was a large Christian community in this city. We also don't read of any false teachers, like the Nicolaitans, infiltrating the fellowship and leading people astray. If you were looking for a church to join, of the seven churches listed here in Revelation, this would likely be the best fit for most Christians living in 21st century America. These people had vision, money, and a relatively secure position in the community. I wonder how many well-known or affluent people were a part of this church. Here was a church people commuted to as they passed by several Philadelphian-type churches, because First Church of Laodicea was obviously doing something right to enjoy such wealth and success. *God's hand of blessing must surely be upon this church,* the people thought.

Think again! As the Lord of the Church gazed upon this fellowship, He threatened to spit it out of His mouth. They were lukewarm and lovin' it!

The city of Laodicea did not have an adequate water supply of its own; consequently, their water was piped in from other places. Of course, by the time the water made it to Laodicea, it was lukewarm. The church of Laodicea was just like their water supply—lukewarm. The Lord of the Church would rather have them be either hot or cold. Now that sounds very odd to our ears. What does He mean by that? Would He prefer that they be honest about their cold spiritual lives, or else be truly red hot about their love for Him? Is that what the Lord means when he judges them for being lukewarm?

I believe Jesus is thinking about Laodicea's two neighboring cities. The city six miles to the north was called Hierapolis; it was known for its hot springs. People came from all over to take a hot bath in its healing waters. In contrast, on the south side of Laodicea was the town of Colossae. It was known for its cold, pure mountain spring water. Nothing was more refreshing after a hot journey than to drink from its cold springs.

Now with this as context, let's return to what Jesus said about Laodicea. Jesus was not condemning them for spiritual tepidness, but rather, for barrenness and selfishness. Laodicea was not like the hot and healing waters of Hierapolis, nor were they like the cold and refreshing waters of Colossae. They had resources and relative peace in their city, but for all of their advantages, they were doing nothing to bring healing and spiritual refreshment to others, either within Laodicea or beyond. They were only thinking about themselves.

What caused this barrenness and complacency? We are given a brief and accurate description of the symptoms of the Laodicean church in chapter 3 of Revelation, verses 17-18. The author describes them as being, wretched, pitiful, poor, blind, and naked. These would have been the least likely descriptions you would have received had you asked the members of the Laodicean church to describe themselves.

The Lord of the Church often sees the conditions of our churches differently than we do. That is why it is always important for church leaders and members alike to ask the Lord to search their hearts and give His true appraisal of our churches. Call Him before you call in the church consultants!

With the symptoms described, the Lord of the Church gave His diagnosis and treatment. The first culprit was self-sufficiency. The Laodicean church believed that they were rich and had all that they needed. Who needs God, and who needs to pray if you believe that you have all the resources you require to meet all of your own needs? If we only do what our own resources allow us to do, we never learn to pray and wait for the Lord to do more than we ask or can even imagine, so that He will receive the glory! Self-sufficient churches are not praying churches. That is why the Lord counsels them to buy gold refined in the fire so, that they can truly become rich.

A second symptom of the Laodicean church was self-deception. They were consumed with their own little kingdoms, deceived into thinking that the Lord was even blessing them. What they needed was eye salve. How ironic that the city of Laodicea was known for its manufacturing of eye salve. What the church of Laodicea needed was God's eye salve!

A final symptom of the church at Laodicea was self-righteousness. Jesus told them that they were naked. Wait a moment! How can rich people, living in the city known for making black wool, be naked? Notice what Jesus told them they needed—white clothes. Throughout Scripture, and particularly in the book of Revelation, white clothes stood for the righteousness that only Christ can give. The Laodiceans were naked. They had nice clothes to wear, but there was not enough money or fine clothes available to cover a heart full of shame, guilt, and misery. Righteousness does not come from anything man can do. Only when one comes to Christ as a sinner on bended knee can he or she receive the white garment of Christ's righteousness. These clothes are given because of what Christ did on the cross, and they can only be appropriated as a gift of grace, received by a humble and repentant heart, through faith. For people who are used to calling all the shots or buying their way through life, this is bitter medicine to swallow.

In every age, there have been movements within the Church to minimize Christ's atonement. Satan always weakens the Church from within by diminishing the person of Christ and the necessity of His sacrifice for our sins. In the eighteenth century, Charles Chauncey, the father of Universalism, diminished the atonement by diminishing the justice and wrath of God. He believed God is too loving to send anyone to hell—at least for an eternity. A similar diminishing of Christ's person and atonement developed among the Unitarians.[66] The result was a self-righteousness tailor-made for skeptical deists and rich sophisticates.

Reflect upon these thoughts and pray.

How would *you* describe *your* church? Now ask the *Lord* to describe *your* church from *His* perspective. As you listen to His words, are there any areas of concern? If so, lift them before the Lord in prayer and ask Him to show you how you can address these concerns, biblically and pastorally.

(Daily reading: Revelation 3:14-22)

Day 23

The School of the Prophets

We have studied the five "unhealthy" churches that the Lord of the Church describes in the book of Revelation. The two "healthy" churches (Smyrna and Philadelphia) are seen as being faithful remnants—albeit small and poor. Both are promised a crown of life if they remain faithful and allow no one to take their crowns. In every age, God preserves a faithful remnant. As we will see today, the preservation of that remnant includes discipleship and persistent mentoring of the next generation of spiritual leaders.

Before Timothy Dwight became president of Yale, another Elijah was sent to rebuild the altars for a whole new generation of spiritual leaders. In 1779, Dr. John Blair Smith became the president of Hampden-Sidney College in Virginia. The college was founded in 1775, and it still exists today as a private all-male college.

The duties of the president of Hampden-Sidney College included pastoring the Cumberland and Briery Presbyterian Churches. This Dr. Smith did until the Revolutionary War when the British invaded Prince Edward County, and the school was forced to suspend classes. Smith raised up a company of volunteers to be a part of the Virginia militia. This company of students and youth from his congregations worked to repel the British invasion of the lower counties of Virginia—with John Blair Smith serving as their captain.

When Dr. Smith ended his service in the army, he continued his work as president of Hampden-Sidney. It was during this time, soon after the war, that a revival broke out in the area among the Baptists and Methodists (an encouraging precursor of what was in store for the country). Dr. Smith, desiring the same revival in his churches, established prayer meetings. Through his zealous and evangelistic preaching, revival came to his two congregations in 1787. However, things were different at the college. The students who returned after the war seemed to be hardened spiritually because of what they had experienced. The students at Hampden-Sidney were careless about their spiritual condition. They were given to drunkenness, cheating, lying, profanity and a mocking contempt of spiritual things.[67]

This animosity toward the Christian Faith reached a fevered pitch when four students gathered for prayer in their room. These four students were so concerned about their own spiritual condition that they would meet out in the woods, in hiding, to read the Bible, discuss spiritual matters, and pray. Their fear of the other students was not unfounded. One Saturday, due to inclement weather, they procured a room in the college for their meeting. They locked the door and began to pray and sing. Someone heard them singing, and soon a frenzied mob gathered at the room, shouting, swearing and banging at the door, demanding entrance to the room. This riot attracted the attention of the college officials who quelled it and brought the parties involved before Dr. Smith who called for an explanation. The following is a detailed report of that meeting with Dr. Smith.

> Some of the ringleaders at once arose, and said, that they heard singing and praying, like the Methodists, in one of the rooms and had broken up the disorderly proceeding. Until that moment neither the President nor the tutors, Lacy and Mahon, had any idea that, besides Cary Allen, there was a praying youth in College. "And who are the culprits?" enquired the President. The four youth confessed themselves guilty of the charge. Looking at them with tears in his eyes, he exclaimed, "Is it possible that some of my students desire to pray, and is it possible that any desire to hinder them? Well

> my young friends, you shall have a place to pray. The next Saturday's prayer-meeting shall be in my parlor, and I will meet with you." At the appointed hour on the next Saturday, the four young men went trembling to the President's parlor; the novelty of the thing had filled the room. They were called on and prayed, each in his turn, and the President gave a warm exhortation. The succeeding Saturday, the whole house was filled to overflowing. The next meeting was in the College Hall, which was filled with students and people from the neighborhood. The revival, which had been heard of in Charlotte and part of Cumberland, was felt in College. Fully half the students were enquiring what they should do to be saved. Prayer meetings were set up forthwith in different parts of Mr. Smith's charge, and the awakening seemed to spread over the two Counties.[68]

All four students and thirty others from this revival went into ministry, and the Lord used them during the Second Great Awakening. Dr. Smith, after being criticized for being more interested in the spread of the gospel than running a college, resigned and eventually became the pastor of Pine Street Presbyterian Church in Philadelphia. His pastoral and evangelistic heart was tested when a yellow fever epidemic hit the city in 1793. Half of the population of Philadelphia fled the city, but Dr. Smith remained to tend the sick, bury the dead, and to preach every Sunday. The Pine Street church was the only church open in the city during the epidemic. Through his faithful leadership, Dr. Blair and his congregation healed the sick and refreshed those who remained behind in the city. Laodicea, it was not!

The 21st century Church will begin to pray fervently for the next great awakening when its leaders and pastors, like Dr. John Blair Smith, begin rebuilding the broken altars for future generations by:

1. Preparing, like Elijah, spending time alone with the Lord at each one's own Brook Cherith, before facing his own spiritual battles on Mt. Carmel.

2. Praying fervently for revival; praying regularly with other pastors and church leaders.
3. Preaching passionately the whole counsel of God's infallible word; walking in that counsel consistently before a watching world and congregation.
4. Pastoring the next generation of spiritual leaders by providing ongoing discipleship and loving encouragement.

Reflect upon these thoughts and pray.

If you are a pastor or a spiritual leader in your church, can you honestly say that these are your four top priorities in ministry? If not, what are your top four priorities? Continue praying for all pastors and pray that seminaries and Bible schools may become, as Jonathan Edwards suggested, nurseries of piety as they prepare the next generation of spiritual leaders.

(Daily reading: I Kings 18:31-46)

If you are a pastor or work in ministry fulltime, are you part of a monthly pastor's prayer group? If so, does your group pray for the outpouring of the Spirit? If there is no such group in your city or community—start one.

The Next Great Awakening

Day 24

Concerts of Prayer

The first half of this book is intentionally negative, and I pray, sharp to the touch. The Lord raised up a faithful and refined remnant who would fervently pray and serve Him. These were people who sought first His kingdom and His righteousness in their own hearts, so they could pray for a fallen nation with God's heart and eyes. We need to change our myopic view of history and realize that our nation has experienced dark and depraved times in its past. Every generation considers the evils of its day to be far greater than the previous generation—*What is this world coming to?* It's a question Adam and Eve may have asked as they viewed the lifeless body of their son Abel.

Our brief forays into the eighteenth century depict a young republic on the verge of collapse. Churches were empty, and pulpits were either preaching an atonement-less gospel or preaching without any passion or conviction. College students and groups of French-loving radicals living in the 1790s make the 1960s' radical student movements and "love-ins" look like Sunday school conventions in comparison. The wild-west gangs of renegades and fugitives of the law might even frighten some of today's urban gangs. The government was just as divided with political bickering and negative campaining as it is today.

Despite the darkness of the times, the Lord preserved a remnant of faithful pastors and churches who didn't give up hope. They began to pray fervently in small groups and even across denominational lines in cities across the country. Encouraged by the "Concerts of Prayer" taking place in England, the American churches began to call their members to what Jonathan Edwards described as the explicit and visible union of God's people in extraordinary prayer for revival. Edwards went on to describe in his work entitled, how, in 1774, a number of ministers in Scottland began this movement, first among themselves, and then they invited all who were concerned about the present state of the Church to gather "socially" and privately for special times of prayer. They proposed to gather in groups on Saturday evenings and early every Sunday morning for prayer near the times of *dispensing gospel ordinances which are the great means, in the use of which God is wont to grant His Spirit to mankind, and the principal means that te Spirit of God makes use of to carry on his work of grace. . .*[69] They also recommended that the first Tuesday of every quarter be set aside for mutual and private prayer and fasting. The orginal call to prayer was for a period of two years; then it was extended for another seven years. They all had agreed not to make this known publically through the press, but rather, through personal correspondence.

As a result, prayer societies formed all across Great Britain and then moved into other countries, including parts of the United States. Jonathan Edwards viewed this movement as a beginning fulfillment of Zechariah 8, verse 21: . . . *and*

> *About five years ago, the concert of prayer proposed to be observed quarterly, and which was attended in many parts of the land, was also set up here, and the members of the church, with some others, attended. These seasons appeared to be solemn, and were animating and encouraging to numbers of God's people. But nothing special appeared, indicating a revival of religion, until January, 1799, when it was noticed that our religious assemblies were more solemn and attentive. The religious people, hearing of some revivals of religion in two or three other towns in the vicinity, and having before this heard of the work of God at a further distance, were induced to hope, and ardently to pray that we might have a gracious visit also.*
>
> *-Rev. Ammi R. Robins, Norfolk Conn.*

the inhabitants of one city will go to another and say, **Let us go at once to entreat the Lord and seek the Lord Almighty.** Forty years later, as times grew more difficult both in England and in the United States, the call for concerts of prayer was once again sounded.

In the United States, Baptist leaders such as Isaac Backus and Stephen Gano, and Congregational leaders in New England issued a call for concerts of prayer. Soon other denominations, such as the Presbyterians and Methodists, issued calls to their congregations to form praying socieities. Churches of every denomination gathered for weekly "union prayer meetings" in their cities and within their own congregations to seek the grace of God and to entreat Him to revive both the Church and the country. As the churches began to pray in concert for another awakening, in 1795 signs of revival were beginning to surface sporatically in some areas of the country.

Is the Lord about to do the same thing today? Do we even want the Lord to move with great power among us? The scalple-like nature of the first 21 days was intended to probe our hearts to determine if we really want another great awakening today? Do you want His refining fire to fall upon your church and upon all of the churches in the United States? Do you want the Lord to transform our culture, including your city and neighborhood? If your heart yearns for revival, then the rest of this book will encourage you to pray fervently and believe that God can send another great awakening based upon His own promises and past answers. This second half will also challenge you to put your zeal to work as you gather others around you to pray and sow the seed of the gospel across this nation.

Reflect upon these thoughts and pray.

How hard would it be for churches in your city to gather together once a month or even once a quarter to pray for the next great awakening? What are some of the obstacles keeping churches from coming together in concerts of prayer? Pray against these obstacles and ask the Lord to begin this good work in your own city.

(Daily reading: Zechariah 8:1-3, 20-22)

Day 25

Give Him No Rest!

What motivates you to keep praying? As you think back upon the times in your life when you prayed with great urgency and zeal, even for days on end, what kept you on your knees praying? When have you been most like the widow in Jesus' parable—you know, the widow who pestered the unjust judge for justice until he finally gave in? There was some adversary who was obviously taking advantage of this widow, and there was no one to turn to for help except this judge. He had the authority to help her, but he did not have the heart to help her, because he *neither feared God nor cared about men* (Luke 18:2). The only reason the widow kept pestering him was due to her helpless situation. The only reason the judge finally gave in to her request was due to her relentless supplication. Like the widow, the times when we relentlessly approach God's throne in prayer are the times when we, too, acknowledge our total helplessness and our total dependence upon the Father.

In this parable, Jesus wants to encourage persistent praying with the assurance that the Father is a just judge. If this judge in the parable finally granted justice, even though he cared nothing about this widow or her needs, how much more will our loving Father readily grant us justice and help in our times of need when we fervently pray to Him!

There is a second motivation to pray that we often skip over in this passage. Jesus concludes the parable with this question: *However, when the Son of Man comes, will he find faith on the earth?* What does the second coming of Christ have to do with persistent praying? The answer is, *faith*. Persistent praying gives evidence of faith. Faith in what? In this context, it is faith that Christ will come again and will bring justice. It is faith in what Christ has promised—that all who seek and pray for His Kingdom to come will not be disappointed.

A revival or a great awakening is but a foretaste of Christ's final coming to establish His kingdom. Christians who fervently pray for spiritual revival in their churches and who pray with boldness for nations and people groups to experience Christ's Kingdom in their lives will not be disappointed! In fact, many Christians are surprised to find that God promises to bring revivals and national awakenings because of fervent praying. He wants us to seek Him in prayer for such things.

One such promise is found in Isaiah 62:6-7, *You who call on the Lord give yourselves no rest, and give him no rest till he establishes Jerusalem and makes her the praise of the earth.* The Jerusalem described here is not one of bricks and mortar. In this passage, Jerusalem refers to God's people—His bride, the Church. It is God's desire for the righteousness and salvation of Jerusalem to shine out like the dawn, or as a blazing torch (62:1) so all the nations of the world will come and bring her praise. As God's people shine like stars in a crooked and depraved generation, they are able to hold out the Word of life (Philippians 2:15). People

> *And here it must be observed, that numbers who had as yet remained unmoved, when they came to witness the solemn scene—when they beheld many of their intimate companions—a husband—a wife—a brother—a sister—a parent—a child—a near friend—a late jovial companion, with sweet serenity, solemnly giving up themselves to the Lord—publicly enlisting under the banner of Jesus, and engaging forever to renounce the ways of sin, and the corrupt practices of the world, and cleave to the Lord—and beholding one and another, at the same time, baptized in his name—they were pierced through, as it were, with a dart. They often went home full of distress, and could never find rest or ease, until they had submitted to a sovereign God, and placed their hope and confidence on Jesus Christ.*
>
> *-Rev Ammi Robbins, Norfolk, Conn (1799)*

become attracted to churches (Jerusalem) when Christians shine with righteousness, and the Spirit of God moves in their midst, bringing salvation even into the hardest of hearts.

The Lord calls all Christians to be watchmen who know the signs of the times and who use their voices like trumpets, warning of danger. They also inspire others to pray fervently—praying for the fulfillment of God's promises. These watchmen, and all who heed their call, are encouraged by God to pester Him night and day, **and then He will** establish Jerusalem and make her the praise of the entire earth.

Reflect upon these thoughts and pray.

Do you believe the promise in Isaiah 62:7 that the Lord will make His Church so radiant that even the most skeptical among us today will be drawn to our church fellowships to experience the presence and power of the Lord? If so, give the Lord no rest until he fulfills this promise in your church and in churches across the country.

Lord, make your Church so radiant that the world will be drawn to You. Begin with my church and transform our fellowship with your presence and power. Amen.

(Daily reading: Isaiah 62:1-2, 6-7)

Day 26

A "Spirit" of Supplication

Zechariah is one of the most encouraging, and sadly, one of the most under-read prophets in all of the Old Testament. Granted, this is a mysterious book to interpret. However, the prophecies contained in this book clearly present future specifics about the coming Messiah. In fact, Zechariah is quoted eleven different times in the New Testament, particularly in the Gospels when Christ is fulfilling Zechariah's prophecies. Here in this prophetic book, which rivals Isaiah's prophecies, we are reminded not to despise the *day of small things* (4:10). When the older exiles looked at the restored temple after it was finished, they grieved, because it did not compare to the former temple built by Solomon. However, a grander and more glorious temple will arise out of this rebuilt temple; Jesus and

> *At the time of my ordination, which was April, 1795, the situation of this church called for the earnest prayers of all who had a heart to pray. The number of its members then was not much greater than it had been for twenty-five years before; and almost the whole of them were bowing under the infirmities of age. No person had been received into it, in the course of sixteen years. To see the youth, all as one, wasting away their best moments in stupidity—to view them as accountable creatures, and yet living apparently without hope—"without a wish beyond the grave"—and to see a few gray-headed persons compose almost the whole number of communicants at the sacramental table—must, to one just entering on the work of ministry, awaken feelings which cannot be easily described.*
>
> *-Rev. Samuel Shepherd, Lenox, Mass (1799)*

all who follow Him will be as stones added to this rising temple. This new temple will not be constructed by human might or power, *but by my Spirit, says the Lord Almighty*. It will be a temple compromised of people from every tribe and people group of the world.

The prophesies of Zechariah take us to Calvary, Pentecost, and even to the "last days," when all of the prophecies will be fulfilled and Christ will return and create a new heaven and earth. It will be a time when even the most mundane things, like bells and cooking pots, will contain the inscription, Holy to the Lord (14:20), as everything will give praise to the Lord and will be used for His glory. It is in this latter section of the book, chapter 12, where Zechariah prophecies about a time about which the Lord says, *I will pour out on the house of David and the inhabitants of Jerusalem a Spirit of grace and supplication. They will look on me, the one they have pierced, and they will mourn for him. . ."* (12:10).

Jonathan Edwards viewed this passage as a key promise to motivate Christians in every age to keep praying. Whenever the Lord has something great to accomplish in His kingdom, he always precedes this work by pouring out His Holy Spirit, Who will give a spirit of grace and supplication to His people. The prayers of the faithful will be accompanied by tears of repentance and cries for forgiveness. Grace and cleansing will follow, as a fountain, washing away all their sin and impurity; the false prophets and impure spirits will be removed from the land (chap.13). This speaks of revival and great awakenings as hearts will be regenerated, and even the land will become transformed as evil spirits and false teachers are removed from their strongholds. Edwards suggests that the Lord must raise up and pour out His spirit of grace and supplication upon the Church to bring about revival, thereby ridding the land of the demonic. If Christ told his disciples, this kind can only come out by prayer and fasting (Mark 9:29), how much more prayer and fasting will be needed by many people to remove the demonic from the land?[70]

Now is the time to pray for the outpouring of the Spirit, while we still can, because a time is coming, according to the book of Revelation, when Christ will return . . . *coming with the clouds, and every eye will see him, even those who pierced him*; and all the peoples of the earth will mourn because of him. So shall it be! Amen (Rev.1:7). When this happens, there will no longer be an opportunity for repentance. At that time, the mission of the Church will cease, and the joy of harvest will begin in earnest.

This passage from Zechariah spoke to my heart and convicted me of a spirit of resignation concerning the state of Church and our country. As a pastor, I felt like many of the pastors who were faithfully serving the Lord in the latter part of the eighteenth century. Why isn't the Church growing? Where are all the young people? Why isn't there more of a spiritual hunger, as there was in earlier years? Why isn't there more commitment to the Lordship of Jesus Christ? If there are a majority of people who still claim to be Christians, why is the culture becoming harsher and more depraved? Why are there so many camps within the Church, questioning every historic doctrine, afraid to take a stand even on moral and ethical issues that the Bible clearly addresses? The list goes on, but for me, I had seen and experienced enough to conclude that we must be living in the last days; therefore, another revival or great awakening was no longer possible. Why even do outreach, if the Lord is about to return? Why stay up all night and worry about people leaving the Church; they obviously never had a relationship with Christ to begin with, because their faith seems to have grown cold, just as Christ predicted would happen in the last days (Matt. 24:10). I concluded that my work as a pastor would now be to focus primarily upon the faithful who were left, preparing them and their children for the tough times ahead and for the future anti-Christ, who would soon appear.

I'm being a bit melodramatic here, but these thoughts and emotions were present in some of my more discouraged moments. The problem with this kind of resignation, however, is that it causes a person to stop praying, both for revival in the land and for Christ's Kingdom to come. When a pastor thinks or even voices this kind of negative view of God's kingdom, its poison can discourage an entire church. It resembles

Elijah's depressed state underneath the broom tree after his great victory on Mt Carmel against the prophets of Baal, *I have had enough, Lord. . . Take my life; I am no better than my ancestors* (I Kings 19:4). We look at our current circumstances from our tiny perspectives, and we, too, are quick to give up hope. We want to shake Elijah and say, *You are not alone! Don't you remember the school of the Prophets? Why discourage them? What about the 7000 others who have not bowed down to Baal?*

Zechariah, chapter 12, encouraged me not to give up. The Lord can still raise-up a spirit of supplication, and His Spirit can still blow and put life back into lifeless churches and sleeping Christians.

Do not despise the day of small things!

Reflect upon these thoughts and pray.

Do you often feel discouraged and tempted to give up praying for revival in the land? How has the Lord encouraged you to keep praying?

Lord, keep me fervently praying for the next great awakening. Bring to my mind and impress upon my heart your many promises of revival. Amen.

(Daily reading: Zechariah 12:10-13:3)

Day 27

Hunger and Thirst for Righteousness

I live near a settlement of Amish. Outside of dodging horse and buggies and the occasional "droppings" left behind on the roads, the Amish are good neighbors. As a lover of history, I am fascinated by watching them farm and live as our forefathers did back in the 1800s. Why do they live this way? There is certainly a great deal of religious legalism permeating their beliefs. Like all forms of legalism, it strangles the joy of grace and the blessed assurance of being righteous in the sight of God through Christ's sacrifice on the cross. To get at the heart of my question, *Why do they choose to live this way?*, we need to dig into their past.

During the Protestant Reformation, a segment of the Protestant Church believed and taught that there should be a total reformation away from the Roman Catholic Church. Along with all the other groups of new Protestant Christians, they believed in all the words of protest Luther nailed upon the doors of Wittenberg Castle. However, their protests went well beyond Luther's issues. They thought the Roman Catholic Church was too involved in the "kingdoms" of this world. They were more interested in living out the Kingdom of Heaven by closely following the teachings of Jesus, to love our enemies and to forgive those who insult us. They were people who wanted to live the Sermon on the Mount, and not just talk about it.

The people who held these beliefs were soon under the leadership and teaching of men like Jakob Amman and Menno Simons. True to their beliefs, they avoided any civil involvement and became pacifists in times of war. This made them hugely unpopular, and many faced persecution by both fellow Protestants and Roman Catholics in Europe.

Eventually, a split took place within their own ranks. Some thought Jakob Amman was too strict, especially with the practice of "shunning" or excommunication. Menno Simons and a more moderate group separated and became what is known as the "Mennonites." The more conservative group became known as "Amish." At the core of both groups was (is) a desire to stay pure and to live out the kingdom of heaven on earth by avoiding as much of this world's kingdoms as possible, living in separate communities that were (are) virtually frozen in space and time.

We can criticize the Amish for being separatists, but will there come a time, or has that time already come, when faithful Christians will be forced to do similar things for their children's sake? Will Christians soon become "Amish-like" when dealing with social media, modern day entertainment, and all other public places where our children and grandchildren live, play and go to school? Is the only solution an Amish one?

They Will Be Satisfied!

We've been looking at God's promises for revival as a way to encourage us on, as we fervently pray for the Lord to move with great power in our midst. As we will see in the days ahead, when the Lord blessed our nation with a great outpouring of His Spirit in the Second Great Awakening, culture changed! Those who hunger and thirst for the righteousness of Christ will be satisfied; no true revival can take place without this Spirit-generated hunger for Christ's righteousness. However, there is another kind of hunger and thirst for righteousness; it is a hunger and thirst for moral and social righteousness in our world. This kind of righteousness means living and loving rightly. This is the total opposite of that which is perverse, false, and self-seeking.

The people praying for revival in the late eighteenth century had a hunger and a thirst for the Lord's righteousness to be the governing principle of every classroom, courtroom, boardroom, and bedroom. They wept while they prayed for a spiritually lethargic Church and a culturally decaying nation. They prayed, *You heavens above, rain down righteousness; let the clouds shower it down. Let the earth open wide, let salvation spring up, let righteousness grow with it;* I the Lord, have created it (Isaiah 45:8). Indeed, the Lord answered their prayers and brought a measure of satisfaction to their souls, as the Spirit rained down upon them; salvation and righteousness sprang up in glorious ways all through the United States, as we will see in our last ten days.

During the height of the Second Great Awakening, righteousness flourished, as cultural temptations diminished, and an environment of godliness became the new norm. People found detestable and shameful the lifestyles, teachings, and forms of entertainment that were previously accepted and praised by society, even by many within the Church. The revival helped people to see their world and society through God's eyes.

Why would anyone want to avoid a society and culture that was flourishing with God's righteousness? Who would be anxious about sending their children to school or out to play, or even to use the technology of the day, if every aspect and sphere of society were governed by people who sought first God's Kingdom and righteousness?

The Lord wants people who hunger and thirst for this! He loves to hear them pray and promises that they will be satisfied!

Reflect upon these thoughts and pray.

How do the other beatitudes help us create a hunger and thirst for righteousness? Why do you suppose the people who hunger and thirst for, and because of, righteousness face persecution?

Lord, create in my heart and in the hearts of everyone in our nation a hunger and a thirst for your righteousness! Amen.

(Daily reading: Matthew 5:1-12)

Day 28

A CEO's Blank Check

Do you know how to pray? This may seem like a strange question to ask this far into a book about prayer. I have encouraged you to pray for your pastor, for your children and grandchildren, for the government, and for a general awakening throughout the country. I have even asked you to listen for God's voice of discernment through prayer. Maybe we should stop here and ask the Lord what one disciple asked of Him in Luke 11:1, *Lord, teach us to pray, just as John taught his disciples.*

I can't begin to imagine what words this disciple heard as he silently approached Jesus in Jesus' special place of prayer. What petitions did this man hear as he stood quietly by Jesus? They prayed aloud in those days, so the man was privy to a portion of Jesus' conversation with the Father, if he indeed were close enough to hear Jesus pray. Something prompted this man to ask Jesus for a lesson on prayer. Maybe it was the fact that Jesus prayed often and alone which caused the man to ask for a lesson on prayer. *There must be something in His prayer life that is far more enjoyable than what I experience in my prayer time.*

Jesus' response to the man reflected the very petitions and intimacy of the prayer he had just interrupted. Jesus tells his disciples to start praying using the word "Abba" or "loving Father" to address the Lord. This was an amazing revelation! This shouldn't be surprising, because the rest of Jesus' lesson on prayer highlights the love and goodness of the Father. Address the Lord with heartfelt intimacy and childlike dependency, as you ask for His Kingdom to come, for your daily needs, for forgiveness, and for strength to say, no, to temptations. The Lord will give you these things, because, *If you then, though you are evil, know how to give good gifts to your children, how much more will your Father in heaven give the Holy Spirit to those who ask him!* (Luke 11:13).

Did you catch that last phrase? Matthew's Gospel has a similar phrase, except he replaces "the Holy Spirit" with the words "good gifts." Luke's words surprise us, because the context is about food and material things. Why does he interject the Holy Spirit here? Certainly, the Spirit is the source of all that is good. Luke writes and places his chapters and verses in a thematic structure to bring home a very important point. After he tells us about the Father's good gift of the Holy Spirit, he moves right into the account of Jesus driving out a demon from a man and proceeds to explain to some of the skeptics who think Jesus is using Satan's power to drive out demons: *If Satan is divided against himself, how can his kingdom stand. . . But if I drive out demons by the finger of God, then the kingdom of God has come to you* (vss.18 & 20). Luke is describing a foretaste of the Kingdom of God, which is a spiritual revolution! For Luke, the "finger of God" is the Holy Spirit (see Matthew 12:28). The revolution is on its way, and the Lord desires us to ask Him for more of it!

Think of it this way. You are the newly elected mayor of a financially bankrupt city—like Detroit. You have wonderful plans and dreams to revitalize the entire city to make it a place where people and businesses want to settle down and call it home. But you don't have the resources to make it happen, and you are up against street gangs and organized crime bosses who are deeply entrenched in the city; they don't want to see your kind of revitalization. Now imagine that a CEO of a very large corporation approaches you and desires the same revitalization of the city that you so desperately want. In fact, this corporate giant has such amazing plans for revitalization that you cannot even imagine or dream that they might be possible. The CEO goes on to tell you that he wants to move his corporate headquarters into your city. That's not all! The CEO tells you, as mayor, that if you need resources to hire additional police, first responders, or anything else to make the city a great place to live, all you need to do is just ask, and you will receive it. There will be an endless supply of resources available to you to revitalize the city. The only thing you need to do is just to ask.

While this may not be a perfect analogy, it does illustrate the promise that Jesus gives to us in Luke, chapter 11, verse 13. If you have a heart for Kingdom-revitalization, both in the Church and in society, the CEO of the entire universe has just given you a blank check. Don't be bashful; keep on asking, seeking, and knocking at His door, asking for even more!

Reflect upon these thoughts and pray.

Do you pray for more of the Holy Spirit in your life? What happens in a person's life when the Holy Spirit is given access to and control of every part of it? Pray the following prayer with boldness and assurance:

Lord, I want the Holy Spirit to be in control of every aspect of my life. It is my heart's desire for the Spirit to revitalize my faith. Amen.

(Daily reading: Luke 11:1-14)

Day 29

The Age of Revivals

How many revivals or Great Awakenings has the Church enjoyed since Pentecost? The answer to that question varies depending upon one's definition of an awakening. In terms of "great awakenings" which have spread across oceans and continents, a minimal list would include: The Reformation, Puritan-Pietism (16th Century), The First Great Awakening, The Second Great Awakening, The 1858-59 Prayer Awakening, and the Welsh Revival in 1904-05. My own answer to this question favors a much larger list, because at Pentecost the Spirit descended and brought us all into the "age" of revivals.

In Joel, chapter 2, the prophet speaks of a *dreadful day of the Lord,* which will cover the entire planet and be accompanied by wonders in the heavens—the sun will be turned to darkness and the moon to blood red. In the immediate context, Joel calls the people to repentance after they experience the swarms of locusts, which will devour their crops. His description of what these locusts will do must have sent chills down their spines. Joel says in chapter 2, verse 6: At the sight of them, nations are in anguish; every face turns pale. All of this is but a preview of what is to come. In other words, *If you think this is horrible, wait until the day of the Lord arrives, and the entire world experiences God's judgment!*

This prophet, like all the others in the Old Testament, also brings a message of comfort and hope. God is just and righteous, but he is also merciful. Before the great and final judgment of the world, the Lord says: *I will pour out My Spirit on all people. Your sons and daughters will prophesy, your old men will dream dreams, your young men will see visions. Even on my servants, both men and women, I will pour out my Spirit in those days* (2:28-29). In the Old Testament times, only leaders such as prophets, priests and kings had a taste of the power of the Holy Spirit. The Lord put His Spirit on someone, and the proof of such a mantle of God's power was the ability to prophesy. You may recall that after King Saul was anointed by Samuel to be Israel's first king, King Saul met up with a group of prophets, and Saul joined in with them, giving prophetic utterances (I Samuel 10:11). Even earlier than Saul, Moses gathered the 70 elders around him, and the Lord put his Spirit on them in order to assist Moses in the work of leading the children of Israel. Young Joshua heard two men in the camp, Eldad and Medad, who were not with Moses at the time, speak with prophetic utterances. He quickly went to Moses in order for Moses to put a stop to it. Moses' classic reply to his young aide was, *Are you jealous for my sake? I wish that all the Lord's people were prophets and that the Lord would put his Spirit on them* (Numbers 11:29). Joel's prophecy in chapter 2 declares that a time is coming when Moses' prayer will be answered beyond what he asked or even imagined. A time is coming when the Spirit will not just be put on people, put the Spirit will be poured out and into all people. And this Spirit will not just rest upon a few individuals but will be poured out to all people—men and women, young and old, slave and free. These people will be given the gift of the Holy Spirit to prepare the entire world for a day of final reckoning. Bible commentator David Prior summarizes it this way, *If individual prophets had the task of taking God's word to a nation at risk of God's judgment, a prophetically inspired people would have the task of taking God's word to a world on the brink of ultimate judgment.*[71]

Peter announced, on the day of Pentecost, that Joel's prophecy and Moses' dream had become a reality. Peter quoted Joel's prophecy almost verbatim until he reached the part that spoke about Mount Zion and Jerusalem. He did not need to quote this part, because he was standing in Jerusalem, and deliverance was happening as the people were "cut to the heart," asking Peter how to be delivered. Peter went on to say, *The promise* (of deliverance and the gift of the Holy Spirit) *is for you and your children and for all who are far off—for all whom the Lord our God will call* (Acts 2:39).

How appropriate it was for the Spirit to fall upon these disciples on the day of Pentecost. In the Jewish calendar of feasts, Pentecost was a celebration of the first fruits of their crops. The Jewish people came to bring their first crops seven weeks after the initial start of harvest. Here on this Pentecost, seven weeks after the death and resurrection of Christ, the disciples began to enjoy the first fruits of the final harvest which is to come (I Cor. 15:20, Eph.1:14).

The gift of the Holy Spirit is available to all the nations of the world—all who call upon Him for salvation. That is why we are still living in the age of revival. The gift of the Holy Spirit is still available; people can still call upon the name of the Lord and enjoy salvation and experience the outpouring of the Spirit in their lives.

We should learn from the example of the Disciples who prayed together in the upper room, waiting for the Holy Spirit to descend upon them. Jesus told them that when the Spirit came, they and all of His people would receive power to be witnesses to the ends of the earth. Will not the Lord also answer the prayers of God's people who gather together and fervently pray for His Spirit to be poured out upon this generation, so they, too, can be His witnesses to the ends of the earth?

The Lord has blessed the United States financially, technologically, and culturally, and, arguably, it has been a blessing to the nations of the world. Just imagine how the Lord could use a spiritually revived Church in the United States to reach out to the last people groups in this world! There are still promises yet to be fulfilled (Matthew 24:14, Romans 11:25). Pray that the Lord will continue to use Christians and churches in the United States to fulfill these final promises.

Reflect upon these thoughts and pray.

Do you think churches in the United States have a global vision for ministry? How can you tell if a church has such a global vision? Does your church?

Lord, pour out your Spirit today in the churches of the United States, igniting them with passion to give, serve, and go to the ends of the earth for your glory and honor. Amen.

(Daily reading: Acts 2:14-41)

Day 30

Young Mills and His Mother

Father Mills, the pastor from Torrington, Connecticut, (see Day 15) was not only a father-mentor to many of the pastors who were also struggling through the 1780s and 90s, but he was also the father of three children, the youngest named Samuel. Samuel Mills, Jr., was born April 21, 1783, and placed in the loving arms of his mother, who had prayed even before he was born that the child would grow up and be used for God's glory.

Young Mills was raised in this Christian home under the loving and prayerful care of his parents. When Samuel turned 15 years of age, the Lord started to make Himself known in the young teen's heart. It was 1798, and the Torrington church was beginning to experience the first fruits of the Second Great Awakening. Many hearts were transformed during this time of revival, including that of young Mills. His spiritual experience came in two parts that occurred within a two-year period. Clearly, these were the most difficult two years of this young man's life.

As we will see in Day 32, the experience of many during this great revival brought them to the gates of hell and back. As the Spirit began His work of transformation, many became awestruck at the glory and majesty of God. They were given spiritual sight to see God for who He is, and, as a result of this sight, they also were made painfully aware of their own sinful hearts and natures. People like young Mills went from an emotional high to one of descending spiritual depression, doubting the mercies of God and wondering, How can a Holy and righteous God love and forgive me? In the process, some even began to hate and rebel against God, blaming Him for opening their eyes to their sin, while seeming to shut the fount of His mercy to bring pardon and relief. This was the spiritual condition of young Samuel Mills after the revival at Torrington.

Unable to find peace in his heart, he decided to work on a farm that had been bequeathed to the Mills family by his mother's family. Here he worked until the winter months when he decided to go to the Litchfield Academy. He briefly returned home for a visit before walking the twelve miles to Litchfield to attend this college-prep school. Just before young Mills left for school, his mother pleaded with him to share his heart with her about his spiritual condition. He spoke words that no mother ever wants to hear, *O that I had never been born! O that I never had been born!*[72] Amidst bitter tears, he confessed to his mother, *I have seen to the very bottom of hell,* concerning his own sinful heart. Samuel Mills left that cold morning still felt no assurance of forgiveness. He left that cold morning with tears running down his cheeks, as he made his way to Litchfield.

The only thing a mother in this situation could do was pray. That is exactly what Samuel Mills' mother did. She entered her closet of prayer and did not leave until God granted her a measure of assurance that her child would surely enjoy His mercies. The account of this mother praying for her wayward child has been an encouragement to many praying parents. It is especially poignant when you consider how and when God answered her prayer. As Samuel was making the twelve-mile journey to Litchfield, the Lord broke through his gloom and appeared to him with such beauty and majesty that young Mills was no longer distressed by God and His sovereignty. He went into the woods and exclaimed with joy, *O glorious Sovereignty, O glorious Sovereignty!* His life was changed from that moment on, as God answered the prayers of his mother who was praying for him while he was walking away.

When young Samuel Mills returned after his winter of schooling, Father Mills could see the change in his young son. He made note of something his son had said, which confirmed his son's acceptance of

God's grace; he said that he could not conceive of any course of life in which to pass the rest of his days that would prove so pleasant as to go and communicate the gospel of salvation to the poor heathen.[73]

As a young man with his entire life ahead of him, he believed the Lord was calling him to fulltime ministry. He left the farm, much in the same way Elisha left to follow Elijah, leaving the plough and never turning back. The same Spirit who called and anointed Elisha for ministry, had called young Mills for ministry to those who "were afar off."

Reflect upon these thoughts and pray.

If you were the parent of young Mills, would you have discouraged him from going on to school for fulltime ministry?

Lord, work in the hearts of young people today and give them a broken heart for the spiritually lost, both in our nation and in the world. Amen.

(Daily reading: II Timothy 1:3-14)

The Next Great Awakening

Day 31

Watchman

Ezekiel the prophet was called to be a watchman on behalf of the people who had been exiled and living in the land of Babylon. Historically, watchmen served a city by standing post on the top of a wall or tower to look for the first signs of important news. They were the 7:00 AM, 6:00 PM or 11:00 PM newscasters of their day. Watchmen were the first line of defense for the city. When enemies were approaching, they sounded the trumpet warning in much the same way that our civil defense sirens blast when a tornado is spotted or when a tsunami is approaching the coastline. These watchmen also spotted runners who either brought good news or bad news—news of defeat or news of victory in battle.

In Ezekiel 33, the Lord called Ezekiel to be a faithful watchman, warning God's people to repent and sharing with them the news of what God was doing or was about to do. In the next chapter, the prophet records that he was given notice of the fall of Jerusalem a day prior to the time that the report of the fall reached the exiles. Before the news arrived, Ezekiel, in his role as faithful watchman, told everyone what had happened. True to form, no one believed him. The Bible describes the way in which the people of Israel regarded Ezekiel, considering him to be *nothing more than one who sings love songs with a beautiful voice and plays an instrument well, for they hear your words but do not put them into practice* (33:32). However, the Lord promised Ezekiel that this time things would be different, assuring him that when the news of Jerusalem's final fall did reach the exiles, and it was as Ezekiel had foretold, *then they will know that a prophet has been among them* (vs.33).

Many of the faithful pastors, teachers, and parents living in the last decade of the eighteenth century could easily sympathize with Ezekiel in his role of prophet-watchman. These faithful Christians continued to sound the warning trumpets from pulpits, classrooms and living rooms, but like Ezekiel, their words went unheeded. Looking back upon this time, present day Christians should find great encouragement from these faithful few who kept preaching, teaching and fervently praying, even though it seemed as if no one was listening—including God. But, God was listening

The Lord started to move in various places around the country in the years 1798-99, just before the general outpouring started in 1800-1801. These initial revivals brought needed encouragement to the faithful who had been fervently praying in concerts of prayer all across the country. In fact, as the awakening continued, the news traveled from town to town, and even state to state. Pastors shared with their colleagues how the Spirit was moving in their respective churches during their pastors' prayer gatherings. These pastors became watchmen as they were asked to preach and share their good news with the churches that had not yet

> *The People of God became more sensible of and affected with the low state of religion, and the dangerous, perishing conditions of sinners. It appeared that God made use of the intelligence we had of the revival of religion in other places to excite a longing and praying for the Lord's returning with power to our languishing churches, that we might experience the displays of his power and grace which he was making in other parts. Desire and prayer for this great favor increased through the following winter in many of our congregations, and in the spring and first part of the summer of 1802 there was a considerable rising of expectation that the Lord would not altogether forsake and pass us by, but that he would favor us with a gracious visitation.*
> *-The Committee of Presbytery, Pittsburg Presbytery 1802*

experienced the outpouring of the Spirit. These reports of what the Spirit was doing in other areas created a holy jealousy among the churches in neighboring areas. Prayer meetings, which previously had been attended by just a handful, now had gatherings with standing room only. In fact, the outpouring of the Spirit often started in these prayer gatherings and then spread through the entire church and geographical area.

It is my heartfelt desire to encourage the 21st century Church to keep praying for the next Great Awakening, reporting on what happenened during the second Great Awakening in these last few devotionals. I want to foster a "holy" jealousy among us, so that we too cry out, Lord, *I want these wonderful things to happen in my church . . . in my family . . . in my neighborhood and city . . . in our country and even throughout the world!*

Ezekiel prophesied about a coming time when God would breathe life into the lifeless bones of a dead army. God would wrap flesh and tendons around these dry, dead bones, and then he would breathe upon them with the breath of life. Only after the breath of the Spirit entered them, from the four winds, would they actually become alive and stand to their feet as a vast army (Ezek. 37:2-10).

We want the same thing to happen in our day. Bringing parts of the Church together as finely tuned organizations or gathering as many new people as possible into our church buildings to maintain traditions isn't the end goal. Just as it was not the end goal in Ezekiel's vision to form an army of lifeless soldiers, it is not our goal to pray for "forms of godliness" without the awakening power of the Holy Spirit. It is our heart's desire for the vision of the Valley of Dry Bones to be repeated in the 21st century. I pray that the next several days will give an encouraging picture of what a vast army of spiritually-regenerated soldiers will look like on their feet.

Reflect upon these thoughts and pray.

There have been countless books, ministries and programs written or designed in the past several years offering "church renewal" to lifeless churches. In your experience, have these efforts put lifeless churches back on their feet? If not, what was missing?

Lord, show us true spiritual renewal in our churches and in our culture today. Encourage us to keep praying by sending messengers-watchmen to us with news of where your Spirit is beginning to move, even now, in our midst. Amen.

(Daily reading: Ezekiel 37:1-14)

Day 32

Solemnity and Attentiveness

There is one phrase that occurs throughout the eyewitness accounts of the Second Great Awakening. Almost without exception, these accounts tell us that when the Spirit was about to be poured out upon a church or a group assembled outdoors, there was a "solemn attentiveness" among those present. Young people who previously had either interrupted sermons or joked around with their friends, sat perfectly still. Adults who habitually closed their ears to the sermon were now sitting on the edge of their seats. For pastors, the labor of preaching was made easy and enjoyable as parishioners eagerly absorbed everything—even crying out for more. What was happening?

> *You might often see a congregation sit with deep solemnity depicted in their countenances, without observing a tear or a sob during the service. This last observation is not made with design to cast odium on such natural expressions of a wounded spirit. But the case was so with us, that most of those who were exercised, were often too deeply impressed to weep. Addresses to the passions, now no longer necessary since the attention was engaged . . . little terror was preached, except what is implied in the doctrines.*
>
> *-Rev Edward D. Griffin New Hartford, Conn. 1799*

As the various accounts of revival unfolded, there seemed to be a common feeling or mood, which eventually affected everyone in attendance, including people who came to church in order to disrupt it. This solemnity seemed to be caused by a greater infusion of

God's presence in the assembly. Rev. James McGready described the meetings in Tennessee: *With Propriety we could adopt the language of the patriarch and say, "The Lord is here; how dreadful is this place! It is none other than the house of God, the very gate of heaven . . ." When the congregation was dismissed, no person seemed to wish to leave the place. The solemnity increased, and conviction seemed to spread from heart to heart.*[74]

Something analogous to Jacob's personal encounter with God at Bethel was experienced by many people in the Second Great Awakening. In the Bible, whenever people experienced a taste of God's glory, there was a two-fold reaction. The first reaction was an overwhelming sense of awe and fear. The Hebrew word for glory (kabod) actually means weight or heaviness. We often use the expression, "This is a weighty matter," when dealing with very important and timely issues. The Hebrew language is very expressive, so the word for heaviness (kabod) reflects the actual feelings or experience of one who has been in the presence of God—usually through a vision, dream, or a special encounter, such as was experienced by both Moses and Elijah.

Rev. Jeremiah Hallock of Canton, Connecticut, confessed: *The solemnity of this season cannot be communicated. It is only known by experience.*[75] Another pastor, trying to describe this solemnity, suggested that the people had the appearance of just returning from the funeral of a family member.[76] He went on to describe the people's attentiveness to God's word, *Many were swift to hear and slow to speak.*

The Spiritual experience described by these eighteenth and early nineteenth century reporters will be hard for us today to comprehend, but let me suggest the following. Whenever there is a national or natural tragedy, people are often glued to their televisions or to their laptops for news. Think back to 9/11. This was a very "heavy" time for our nation. If you were like me, you went home and sat in front of the television for the rest of the day and well into the evening. All of us were overwhelmed by the sheer loss of life, and we were fearful that more attacks were imminent. Even the major networks kept broadcasting without taking a break for a commercial. There was no need for fancy graphics, loud music, or a comedy monologue to keep our attention. No, we were fearful, grieved, shocked, speechless and unwaveringly attentive to each and every newscaster who had something new to tell us.

When God visited the churches with His presence and power during the Second Great Awakening, the first sign of His doing so was a heavy solemnity and attentiveness to His word as God's people were assembled together. This was, and is, something that cannot be humanly planned or programmed in a worship service. No matter how emotive the preacher, or how musically gifted the worship leaders are, man cannot reproduce this experience. It is a gift that only God can give to His Church.

Reflect upon these thoughts and pray.

What were you thinking or feeling on 9/11? Were you as glued to the television and the news broadcasts of 9/11 as was the author? Now imagine people in your church with that same solemn attentiveness towards God's word.

Lord, pour out your Spirit upon us today. We want to experience Your presence in our churches in the same way as we received the newscasters during the tragedy of 9/11, so that Your people will hang on Your every word. Amen.

(Daily reading: Genesis 28:10-22)

Day 33

Conviction and Conversion

When the people encountered the glory of God as His Spirit was poured out upon the churches, there was an initial feeling of awe and fear which was hard to explain, and could only be experienced. This experience of awe soon turned to a deep conviction of sin. As the Spirit began this powerful work, the reaction of the people was similar to that of Isaiah, the prophet, who fell down and cried out, *Woe to me. I am ruined! For I am a man of unclean lips, and I live among a people of unclean lips, and my eyes have seen the King, the Lord Almighty* (Isaiah 6:5). In fact, the greater the solemnity within their meetings, the greater the conviction of sin was felt among the people.

> *There on the edge of a prairie in Logan County, KY, the multitudes came together and continued a number of days and nights encamped on the ground, during which time worship was carried on in some part of the encampment. The scene was new to me and passing strange. It baffled description. Many, very many, fell down as men slain in battle, and continued for hours together in an apparently breathless and motionless state, sometimes for a few moments reviving and exhibiting symptoms of life by a deep groan or piercing shriek, or by a prayer for mercy fervently uttered. After lying for hours they obtained deliverance. The gloomy cloud that had covered their faces seemed gradually and visibly to disappear, and hope, in smiles, brightened into joy.*
>
> *-Rev. Barton Stone, Kentucky 1801*

This deep conviction began with a personal

view of one's own sin in the light of God's glory, and a humble confession that God would be right and just to punish them and the entire world for their offenses and the corruption of the world. The people of God also became convicted of ingratitude concerning all of God's daily mercies to them. Rev. Edward Griffin from New Hartford, Connecticut, described this conviction as, . . . those views and feelings which are caused by uncovered truth, and the influence of the Spirit antecedently to conversion.[77] The Spirit revealed the proud and self-righteous hearts of many people, even those who were long-time church members. A man from Tennessee cried out, *I have been a sober professor, I have been a communicant; O, I have been deceived, I have no religion.*[78] Under this conviction, the Spirit basically emptied out the "closet of the heart," revealing every hidden sin, age-old animosity, and selfish idol before their very eyes. The reaction to such a personal disclosure varied. In New England and the Western areas, such as New York and Pennsylvania, people refused to leave church until they found peace in their hearts. In some cases, people remained all through the night, and even for days, before they left, or were encouraged to leave. The young people were often the first to be affected. In Pennsylvania:

> Two young persons who had retired to the woods to pray fell to the ground, unable to bear up any longer under the distressing anguish of a wounded spirit. Their cries for mercy were very affecting. After some time, two persons went to them and inquired the cause of their distress. Their reply was that they were exposed to the wrath of God. When Christ was proposed to them as a remedy, their reply was that their hearts were at enmity against God, and they could not accept him, although they were sure they would be damned without an interest in him; besides, they had so long rejected salvation, they were now afraid God would not have mercy on them.[79]

In the South, the reactions were more vocal, and even more dramatic. This was the dawn of religious "camp-meetings," as thousands of people gathered in outdoor areas to hear preachers from several churches and denominations preach for hours and days on end. It was often during these meetings, especially in Kentucky, that people reacted by falling to the ground, motionless for hours, until they reached a point of deliverance. In some cases, where there was little or no control by the attending pastors, Satan crept into these larger gatherings to discredit the revival as people displayed abnormal reactions such as shrieks, head bobbing, jerks, barking, and hysterical laughter. However, in most of the country, the revival came in stillness, and with great self-examination.

It was the enjoyable, albeit, exhausting work of pastors and other spiritual leaders to help the convicted find their hope and deliverance in Christ. Some would quickly transition from sin and hopelessness to joy as they began to view the infinite love of God, who gave His son, and the infinite love of the Son, who sacrificed His life on the cross. By faith, they received the gift of salvation and began to enjoy the new life of conversion. For other people, the transition took days, weeks, and sometimes even months (i.e., Samuel Mills), before they were given the gift of faith and were able to rejoice with glorious new hope.

Young and old alike sought after the righteousness of Christ. They prayed, read the Scriptures, and often attended every spiritual gathering or worship service that was offered to them in order to hear God's word of assurance. Even young children were brought under conviction. In Ohio, a school of thirty children suspended their recess time and all of their playtime after school in order to read the Bible, talk with each other about the concern of their souls, and then retire into the woods for personal prayer.[80]

Wherever the Spirit was moving, a conviction of sin and unrighteousness tormented many people, placing them in what Bunyan described as the "Slough of Despond" in his book, Pilgrim's Progress. The following is a description of an 18-year-old farm boy from the town of Killingworth, Connecticut, who was the very first convert in that town after the Lord poured out His Spirit during the Second Great Awakening.

From my earliest age, I endeavored to lead a moral life, being often taught that God would punish sinners; but I did not believe that I should suffer for the few offences of which I had been guilty. Having avoided many sins which I saw in others, I imagined all was well with me, till I was about eighteen years old, when I heard a sermon preached upon the necessity of regeneration, which put me upon thinking of the need of a change of heart in myself. I did not, however, well receive the discourse at the time, for I was sensible. I knew nothing about such a change; neither did I wish to know, for I believed myself as good as others without it, and to be equal with them, I thought would be sufficient. However, the thought troubled me considerably from day to day, and caused me to think of praying, which I had never done, except repeating some form as a little child, and doing it to remove the stings of a guilty conscience, when I considered myself in imminent danger. Sometime after this, I heard another sermon that convinced me I had quenched the Spirit, which occasioned me the most alarming fears that I should forever be left to eat the fruit of my own ways. Supposing I was alone in the thoughts of eternity, I separated myself from all company, and determined to seek an interest in Christ. I concluded something must be done to appease God's anger. I read and prayed, and strove in every possible way to prepare myself to go to God that I might be saved from his wrath. The more I strove in this selfish way, the more anxious I was, and no hope was given. Soon I began to murmur and repine, and accused God of the greatest injustice in requiring me to return to him; and while I was striving with all my might, as I supposed, he appeared not to regard me. I considered God obligated to love me, because I had done so much for him, and finding no relief, I wished that he might not be, and began really to doubt the truths of his holy word, and to disbelieve his existence; for if there was a God, I perfectly hated him. I searched the scriptures daily, hoping to find inconsistencies in them, to condemn the Bible because it was against me; and while I was diligently pursuing my purpose, everything I read, and every sermon I heard, condemned me. Christian conversation gave me the most painful sensations. I tried to repent, but I could not feel the least sorrow for my innumerable sins. By endeavoring to repent, I saw my heart still remained impenitent. Although I knew I hated everything serious, yet I determined to habituate myself to the duties which God required, and see if I could not by that means be made to love him, and I continued in this state some months. The fear of having committed the unpardonable sin now began to rise in my mind, and I could find no rest day nor night. When my weary limbs demanded sleep, the fear of awaking in a miserable eternity prevented the closing of my eyes, and nothing gave me ease. No voice of mirth or sound whatever was heard, but what reminded me of the awful day when God shall bring every work into judgment. All self-righteousness failed me; and having no confidence in God, I was left in deep despondency. After a while, a surprising tremor seized all my limbs, and death appeared to have taken hold upon me. Eternity, the word eternity, sounded louder than any voice I ever heard, and every moment of time seemed more valuable than all the wealth of the world. Not long after this, an unusual calmness pervaded my soul, which I thought little of at first, except that I was freed from my awful convictions, and this sometimes grieved me, fearing I had lost all conviction. Soon after, hearing the feelings of a Christian described, I took courage, and thought I knew by experience what they were. The character of God, and the doctrines of the Bible which I could not meditate upon before without hatred, especially those of election and free grace, now appear delightful, and the only means by which, through grace, dead

> sinners can be made the living sons of God. My heart feels its sinfulness. To confess my sins to God, gives me that peace which before I knew nothing of. To sorrow for it, affords that joy which my tongue cannot express. Were I sensible that at death, my hope would perish, yet it seemeth to me now, that I could not willingly quit the service of God, nor the company of Christians; but my unfaithfulness often makes me fear my sincerity; and should I at last be raised to glory, all the praise will be to God for the exhibition of his sovereign grace.[81]

As difficult as this man's journey was, from conviction to conversion, the Lord would use this experience in the life of Asahel Nettleton to prepare him to help countless others in the future to seek the same mercy and grace that he had received from the Lord.

Reflect upon these thoughts and pray.

How would you have counseled this young 18-year-old man who was under conviction? In our attempts to lead people to Christ these days, are we quick to minimize sin, God's holiness, righteousness, and justice, while we maximize God's love and forgiveness? How does this unbalanced view cheapen Christ's sacrifice on the cross?

Lord, we ask that you bring conviction into the hearts of people across this nation as they attend church this week. Holy Spirit, convict the world of guilt in regard to their sin and lack of righteousness, starting within your Church. Amen

(Daily reading: Isaiah 6:1-8)

Has the Lord led you to a prayer group in your church? If not, ask the Lord to lead you to like-minded people within your church and begin praying for every service and for your pastor(s).

Day 34

And the Crocuses Bloomed!

Miracles happen in deserts whenever substantial rain falls. Lifeless and barren landscapes come to life in carpets of green plants and small wild flowers, like the desert crocus. The rocky and windswept sands become a canvas for these beautiful flowers that glisten with the morning dew as the sun rises over the desert. Where did these flowers come from? Who planted these seeds in a lifeless desert?

Some of these dormant seeds were scattered by the winds as they fell from their mother plants. Others were carried by animals in a variety of ways. It is interesting to note that, in the case of crocuses and daffodils (which are the two likely candidates for the flowers mentioned in Isaiah 35:1), they do not produce seeds that fall from the plant and blow around. They grow from bulbs or corms that divide and need to be transplanted. They are dependent upon some outside agent to place them in a fertile and hospitable climate, if they are to have any hope of germination. It truly is a miracle to see these kinds of flowers bloom in the desert.

The Second Great Awakening was like a spring rain in a very parched land. As Christian parents and church leaders prayerfully sought to propagate their faith to the next generation, it seemed to many to be like planting bulbs in the desert. With such a hostile environment, it would take a miracle to produce a harvest of young blooming flowers! But, the rains of God's grace were poured out upon the spiritual desert, in what was a partial fulfillment of Isaiah 35. The prophet foresaw a time when the desert would turn into a blooming garden where even dormant seeds would germinate and blossom. Unlike the desert of God's judgment when man turns away from the Lord (Chap. 34), a new Eden will develop when man returns to the Lord. Isaiah's prophesy goes well beyond God's promise of returning the exiles back to the Promised Land. The prophecy points us to Christ, who is the Highway back to God called, "The Way of Holiness" (vs.8). He is the One who will open the eyes of the blind and heal the deaf, lame and mute (vss.5-6). He will bring rivers of living water to dead and dry hearts (vss.6-7). The recipients of such redemption will enter into Zion (the presence of God) with everlasting joy crowning their heads (vs.10).

Ultimately, this prophesy points us to Christ's return and our final redemption. But wherever Christ's Kingdom comes, a bit of Isaiah 35 is enjoyed as deserts bloom with new life and dormant seeds which were planted, even years earlier, begin to bloom.

The desert of the late eighteenth century bloomed as the Lord poured out His Spirit upon the land. There was no greater evidence of this than in the hearts of rebellious teens and prodigal adults who had openly turned their backs on the Christian Faith. It has often been noted that some of the most virulent atheists have been people that were raised in Christian homes and were participants in the Christian community. This was certainly the case in the eighteenth century.

As the rains of the Holy Spirit started to fall and bring revival, one of the most beautiful sights to see were these very obstinate young people and adults now seeking the Lord with all of their hearts! In the spiritual desert that Thomas Paine, Ethan Allen, Charles Chauncey and the French philosophers tried to create within the American youth culture, new spiritual life was blooming, as young people flocked to church services, special lectures, and small prayer groups. Rev. Joseph Washburn of Farmington, Connecticut, reported that his house became one of the most popular places in town for the young people to gather. Daily they came to him inquiring how to find peace in their hearts. In Plymouth, Connecticut, Rev. Samuel Waterman reported similar happenings among the youth of his town. He wrote that youth, ages 8-18, were meeting together on a weekly basis to pray, read the Bible, sing, and talk about spiritual things. These young people, around forty in all, wanted Rev. Waterman to meet with them. He did this and committed to keep meeting with them. The attendance at these meetings kept growing; in the second week, the forty young people grew to be eighty. Within a couple of weeks, the group had outgrown the house where they were meeting, with over 140 young people in attendance. This huge interest in spiritual matters was amazing to Rev. Waterman, and he wrote: *Although it was now the busiest season of the year, with farmers being about harvest time and the evenings growing short, young men, women and children came from a distance of several miles.*[82]

In Lennox, Massachusetts, a new dance school was about to open. Concerned parents and pastors discouraged dancing schools, because they prepared young people for the dance "balls" which were quickly degenerating into occasions for young people to drink to excess and to get into brawls. There was also a growing number of French dance instructors, especially in the "French-friendly" states like Virginia. One of the most popular French dances was called a "carmagnole," and it accompanied a French Revolution song by the same name. The song and dance were violent, which is why it had become a symbol of the Jacobin rebellion in France. However, in the town of Lennox, the new dance school was aborted, because the young people lost interest in attending. Rev. Giles Cowles rejoiced over the change in the young people in his town, as the Lord poured out His Spirit upon the people of Lennox. Many of the young people who had stopped coming to church were now flocking to every service, as they abandoned their card playing and dances.[83]

The young adults who had defiantly left the faith of their parents and had become deists or even hardened atheists, were aware of the awakening going on around them. They heard the testimonies of revived townsfolk and read about the huge crowds of people who were gathering around the country in the camp meetings. However, many of these young adults stubbornly tried to block the rain from germinating the seed of the gospel that had been planted in their hearts and minds as children. These prodigals endured their own "dark night of the soul," as they were "kicking against the goads" (Acts 26:14). In Canton, Connecticut, a man in his forties refused to attend any of the services during the time of revival. Friends and neighbors eagerly, or in some cases curiously, went to the meetings. Yet, this man stubbornly refused to go. One evening, having gone to bed as uncaring as ever about spiritual matters, he was awakened about midnight when the Spirit brought to his mind the words from Deuteronomy 32:29—words planted in his mind from some earlier reading of the Bible or from a sermon, **O that they were wise, that they would consider their latter ends.** Here was the beginning of the conviction that eventually brought this prodigal home.[84]

The Lord's "rain" was so powerful that entire towns could not escape the presence of the Lord. In Norfolk, Connecticut, a great and universal solemnity fell upon the entire community, seizing the minds and hearts of nearly every person. *It was sufficient to make even an atheist tremble,*[85] according to Rev. Ammi Robbins.

Clearly, the Spirit moved with great power, as countless prodigals began a journey on "the Way of Holiness." Oh, how great was the rejoicing of parents and Christian leaders, who had fervently prayed for that day to come! In addition, as we will read tomorrow, these prodigals returned to churches that were dynamic places of God's grace. No prodigal felt awkward returning, because they returned to fellowships where even the "eldest brother or sister," the ones who had never left the church physically, had also returned to the Lord spiritually, marveling that God would forgive their sins.

Reflect upon these things and pray.

Imagine what our present culture would look like if young people sought the Lord with the same zeal as the children, teens and young adults did during the Second Great Awakening. Imagine what this media savvy generation could accomplish for the Kingdom worldwide, if the same percentage of young people today came to Christ as they did during the Second Great Awakening.

Lord, we are jealous of how you poured out your Spirit upon the youth and the many hard-hearted prodigals during the Second Great Awakening. We implore You to do the same thing today. Gather the young people together in homes to pray, sing, study your word and seek You with all of their hearts. Move in the hearts of our prodigals—give them no rest until they find their rest and peace in You. Amen

(Daily reading: Isaiah 35)

Day 35

A Feasting on the Word

Have you ever attended a football or basketball game when during the last fifteen to twenty minutes of the game, everyone was leaving? If a team is losing by huge numbers in the last quarter, there will always be people who leave early. They don't want to stick around to the bitter end, because they think they know how the game is going to end. These people don't want to witness the dismal defeat of their team. After all, they have enough failure in their own lives; why should they be party to yet another loss—albeit vicarious? They also want to beat the crowds out of the stands and parking lots.

However, if you look around the stadium or field in those latter moments of the game, there are always a few loyal fans who will remain to the bitter end. They are the ones who will receive more than they expected, when their team begins to turn the game around in the last few minutes. These faithful few will stand to their feet and cheer with even greater joy and excitement than they had when their team was competitive in the first part of the game. As their team advances and begins to pull off a miracle, hope is rekindled in the heart of the guy who spent the better part of the morning painting his upper torso with his team's colors.

As we read the accounts of revival in the various churches of the Second Great Awakening, there was this same kind of rekindled hope and renewed joy in the hearts of the faithful who longed to see another great awakening. We've already noted the many faithful who were still in their pews and on their knees, praying and waiting for the Lord to move in what seemed to be the final few minutes of the Church's influence in the United States. Who can forget the sad and dismal report from Rev. Samuel Shepherd of Lenox, Massachusetts (Day 26), who wept over the fact that there were no children in his church and that not a single new person had joined the church in over sixteen years. A melancholy mood crept into the hearts of the members, as one-by-one, the elderly members passed away, and the growing fear that there would no longer be a church in Lenox became a real possibility.

But, as these churches tasted the power of the Spirit in their congregations and towns, the churches became transformed and filled with new excitement. Many of the churches reported that the faithful few who remained were "refreshed," and their hope was rekindled. The Presbyterians reported that the church members who remained in their churches were refreshed, and they enjoyed great consolation from the presence of the Lord.[86] In the Lenox congregation, within the months of revival, fifty-three persons were received into the fellowship. For many of the faithful who had remained in the church over the years, this was the very first time they had witnessed a young person publically engaged in worship with them. The congregation rejoiced as they were given a "prelibation of heavenly joys."[87]

As the faithful were refreshed, the new Christians who were added relished the opportunity to speak of God's grace to others. In fact, there was a new and greater openness to speak of spiritual things within the church and even within the greater community. In Torrington, Connecticut, it was common to hear people in the streets talking about spiritual matters with their neighbors. It was even common to hear visitors from other towns speak about spiritual matters to complete strangers who would then reciprocate and share what the Lord was doing in their lives.[88] This personal sharing of faith developed a unity among Christians from various denominations. With a sense of humility and meekness, many people looked beyond theological differences and viewed others through eyes of grace. Even pastors united in blessed harmony as they shared preaching opportunities in the open-air camp meetings and as they continued to pray together in citywide concerts of prayer. In an open-air camp meeting, six to seven thousand people came and were ministered to by fourteen Presbyterian pastors and eleven pastors from other denominations.[89]

A New Book!

Another wonderful blessing that resembled the early Church of Acts was the devotion and hunger for God's word that became evident. For many who were raised in the Church or had some familiarity with the Bible, the common phrase among awakened Christians was that the Bible became a "New Book" to them. They read God's word with new, redeemed eyes and desired to study it as often as possible. Heads of families gathered their children together for daily prayer and the reading of God's word.

Church services on Sundays were packed, often with standing-room-only crowds. There was such a hunger for God's word that the people cried out for more meetings and for spiritual conferences during the week. In Plymouth, Connecticut, a Sunday evening lecture was added which was the first publically attended evening religious meeting in that town.[90]

Not only were the meetings well attended, but people came from great distances, often through very inclement weather or during some of the busiest times of the year.

The service of God is now sweet and pleasant to them, in all its branches. They love to read God's Word. Many have said the Bible is entirely a new book to them. The perusal of it, which afforded them no satisfaction before, now yields them the highest delight. Now they search the Scriptures daily, and say with the Psalmist, 'O how love I thy law; it is daily my delight.' Those that rarely came to the house of God, are constantly attendants. They love the sanctuary of God, the place where his honor dwelleth, and the delight in the ordinances of the gospel.

-Rev. Rufus Hawley, 1799 Avon, Conn.

In Torrington, Connecticut, the people came through bad weather and over terrible roads to sit for two or three hours, soaking up every word; it was difficult to persuade them to go home even when it was getting late at night.[91]

When the Lord poured out His Spirit during the Second Great Awakening, hearts began to burn as people read the Bible for themselves, and as they became attentive to the preached word of God. What was only head knowledge before, became heart knowledge, as people began to see that everything in the Bible was true. Its words sliced through every excuse, façade and bitterness and reached into the hidden "marrow" of their hearts.

The famine of the word came to an end during the Second Great Awakening and was replaced by a grand feast. As we will see in Day 38, this new hunger created an enormous need for the printing of Bibles and other biblical materials. Oh, how heaven must have exploded with rejoicing, as the works of Thomas Paine became kindling for the hearth, and God's word and Spirit kindled a spiritual fire in the hearts of an awakened America!

Reflect upon these thoughts and pray.

Compare the life of the early Church with what you now know about the awakened churches of the Second Great Awakening. What are the similarities? What's still missing among the churches of the Second Great Awakening?

Lord, as we read about these awakened churches, we long to enjoy the same spirit of unity, love, humility and transparency in our own fellowships. Give this nation a hunger for your word beginning in your Church. Amen.

(Daily reading: Acts 2:42-47)

As a pastor, has the Lord brought to your attention other pastors in your area who are praying together for another great awakening? If not, ask the Lord to lead pastors to you to begin such a concert of prayer.

Day 36

Go! Sow! . . . and Grow!

In my role as the executive director of Project Philip Ministries, it seems like I'm always defending the New Testament model of evangelism. There are many churches today that are still working with the Old Testament model—bring the nations to Jerusalem to meet God. These churches call their members to bring people to church in order to meet God through a worship service or some other event where they can hear the gospel message articulated in a simple way. But is this the New Testament model?

Up until the time recorded in Acts 8, the Church had been meeting in Jerusalem, probably in many small churches located throughout the city. I have seen some estimates that suggest upwards of 20,000 Christians were living in the city at that time. They were growing together, enjoying one another's fellowship, sharing each other's gifts and resources, and they were daily adding new people to their fellowship. However, Jesus' Great Commission was outward-focused—not Jerusalem-focused. Jerusalem was the first off-ramp to a world-wide highway.

The persecution that arose after the death of Stephen put the Church back on the highway, as Christians left the city and scattered the word of God everywhere they went. Philip, our ministry's namesake, went to Samaria and there explained the gospel to an Ethiopian Eunuch, who then took the gospel further down the highway. Christians are meant to "go," leaving their church fellowships in order to "sow" the seed of the gospel message in the fields—starting at home and then moving out to the ends of the earth.

We saw this pattern develop among the awakened Church of the late 18th and early 19th centuries. After people were awakened through the regenerating power of the Holy Spirit, almost all responded with great joy, humility, and a deep sense of the worth of an immortal soul. These responses were the catalysts that sparked a spontaneous expansion of the Church

As we noted in Days 32 and 33, when the Lord poured out His Spirit among the people, they experienced a deep sense of God's presence, which created a holy fear and a conviction of their sin and unworthiness, just as Isaiah had experienced when he had a vision of being in the throne room of God. Daniel and Ezekiel described similar feelings, as did John, when he was given the book of Revelation. Many people were left with a powerful impression of God's majesty, holiness and righteousness. When the Spirit finally gave them a converted heart, their new heart's desire was to reflect Christ's glory and to bring glory and honor to His name. They wanted to live holy and pleasing lives before others, so as not to tarnish the name of the One they had come to love deeply with all of their heart, soul, mind, and strength. In addition, these people began to pray more earnestly for others, since they had a new understanding of the worth and preciousness of the human soul. With ardent love, many began to pray fervently that their families, friends, and neighbors would also be given the same new life that they now enjoyed.

> *The subjects of this work appear to be very sensible of the necessity of Sanctification as well as Justification, and that 'without holiness no man can see the Lord' to be greatly desirous that they themselves and 'all that name the name of Christ should depart from iniquity,' should recommend the religion of Jesus to the consciences and esteem of their fellow men, that the light of their holy conversation should so shine before men that they, seeing their good works, might give glory to God.*
>
> *-Rev. David Rice, 1803 Sermon preached at the opening of the Presbyterian Synod of Kentucky*

Rev. Charles Backus from Somers,

Connecticut, reported that when people decided to join his church in a public profession of faith, it was common for him to hear these people say, *We know not how to refrain from publically appearing on the Lord's side; but we tremble at the thought of reflecting dishonor to his name.*[92]

It was an encouraging surprise for pastors to see the new boldness with which these new Christians spoke to others about their faith and how they implored others to seek the Lord. Rev. Samuel Ralston of Alleghany County, Pennsylvania, wrote: *Many who could not relish any religious conversation are now only delighted when talking about the plan of salvation and the wonders of redeeming love; and many, very many, give evidence by their life and conversation that they are born of God.*[93] Even the young people witnessed to their faith with great passion. In Pennsylvania, the young people began to show remarkable concern for others, and frequently addressed them about the perishing condition they were in, the glories of the Savior, and the excellency and suitableness of the plan of salvation. They warned, invited and pressed sinners to come to Christ, all this in a manner quite astonishing for their years.

Of course, witnessing the changed lives of so many who had previously been opposed to Christianity brought the curious to church services, open air camp meetings, and the many small group "conferences" which were being held in various homes throughout the towns that were experiencing

> *Somewhere between 1800 and 1801, in the upper part of Kentucky, at a memorable place called "Cane Ridge", there was appointed a sacramental meeting by some of the Presbyterian ministers, at which meeting, seemingly unexpected by ministers or people, the mighty power of God was displayed in a very extraordinary manner; many were moved to tears, and bitter and loud crying for mercy. The meeting was protracted for weeks. Ministers of almost all denominations flocked from far and near. The meeting was kept up by night and day. Thousands heard of the mighty work, and came on foot, on horseback, in carriages and wagons. It was supposed that there were in attendance at times during the meeting from twelve to twenty-five thousand people.*
>
> *-Peter Cartwright, Methodist evangelist*

revival. It must be said, though, that this curiosity was also fueled by the Spirit working in their hearts, leading them to find redemption and peace. The camp meetings in Kentucky drew thousands of people from the backwoods, where churches were scarce and the spiritual needs great, because many of the pastors who were "serving" churches were either Universalists or drunks.[94] The Cane Ridge meeting was one of the first of these camp meetings. Originally organized as an area-wide communion service for the scattered Presbyterians in the area, the meeting became a powerful event that actually attracted people from the entire area, as the news of it spread from cabin to cabin.

As new believers were added to the Kingdom in the western and southern states, it became obvious to many denominational leaders that there weren't enough trained pastors to meet the growing demand of the new groups of Christians wanting to form churches and grow in their faith. In 1802, the states of Kentucky and Tennessee had a combined population of 325,000, of whom two-thirds lived in Kentucky. Where would these new pastors and spiritual leaders come from, when so many of the colleges at that time were filled with students who were infatuated with the teachings of Thomas Paine and everything French? In addition, what about the greater commission the Lord gave His church to preach the gospel to the ends of the earth? There were Indian tribes among them who needed to hear the gospel message and who needed to see and experience true examples of white people living the life of Christ among them. Who would go to them as the next generation of missionaries, like David Brainerd, preaching the gospel to them and to the multitudes around the world? The Sovereign Lord was already working on this problem, as we will see in Day 37.

Reflect upon these thoughts and pray.

Do you agree with the author that too many of our churches are not actively sowing the seed of the gospel outside of our church fellowships? If you agree, what are the reasons for it?

Lord, we too desire a fellowship of Christians who are so excited about their faith that they don't hesitate to share it with the world. Pour out your Spirit upon your people with power and grace, so that our lives reflect Your glory, and the testimonies we share will bring glory and honor to Your name. Amen.

(Daily reading: Acts 8)

Day 37

Colleges for Christ!

When we last left Timothy Dwight, the new president of Yale College had challenged the students to an Elijah-type showdown in the debate class. As you recall from Day 5, schools like Yale were filled with students who were calling each other by the first name of their favorite French philosophers, i.e., Voltaire, Rousseau, etc. On some campuses, college students were even burning Bibles and threatening other students who went to church.

> *In the spring and summer of 1802, the revival, in its triumphant progress on the right hand and the left, reached Yale College; and there it came with such power as had never been witnessed within those walls before. It was in the freshman year of my own class. It was like a mighty rushing wind. The whole college was shaken. It seemed for a time as if the whole mass of the students would press into the kingdom. It was the Lord's doing, and marvelous in all eyes. Oh what a blessed change! As the fruit of this revival, so memorable in the history of the institution, fifty eight were added to the college church, and others, I know not how many, joined the churches at home.*
>
> *-Heman Humphrey*

At Yale, Dwight's challenge to the students was simple: Using the same principles of debate and logic, disprove the existence of God and the teachings of the Bible. As hard as they tried to reason and call down fire from France, they were unable to stand up to Dwight's impressive defense of the Christian Faith. Dwight proved himself a worthy opponent. He continued his relentless attacks upon infidelity and deism in his noontime chapel addresses, which were becoming very popular at Yale. In the process, he was grounding these students biblically and theologically, preparing them to be the next generation of pastors, teachers, statesmen, and professional leaders. He was doing what many faithful pastors and parents were striving to do—rebuild the altars, so fire could fall from heaven.

Not all of the colleges had a Timothy Dwight as president. There were still schools where the Christian Faith was held in contempt. It was in these schools that the Lord raised up a handful of faithful students who were led to pray fervently for their fellow students. These small student-led groups of Christians supported each other in the faith, prayed for each other, and provided much needed fellowship in a toxic environment. Sadly, many of these groups on the campuses of Harvard, Dartmouth, Brown, and Andover were small and secretive for fear of being mocked or even physically threatened.

As the Spirit started to awaken the churches in New England, and into New York and Pennsylvania, parents began praying for their college age young people. When the revival broke out at Yale during the 1801-1802 school year, these small prayer groups on other college campuses were greatly encouraged to keep praying—yielding much fruit in the years ahead.

The number of student conversions on these formerly "infidel-infested" campuses is nothing short of miraculous. At Yale College in 1802, 75 out of 230 students were converted; nearly half of these gave themselves to fulltime ministry. Heman Humphrey reported that the triennial catalogue showed that for many years there had been but a few in the seminary preparing for the pulpit. In the four preceding classes, only thirteen names of ministers stand against sixty-nine in the next four years; nearly, if not quite all of them, were brought in by the Great Revival.[95]

The numbers are just as impressive for many of the other colleges.

Many reported the conversion of from one third to over one-half of their student bodies.[96] At Princeton by 1815, over half of the graduating students became ministers of the gospel, serving various denominations in both revived churches and new frontier church plants.

Faithful leaders, such as Timothy Dwight and Dr. John Blair Smith (Day 23), were used to prepare these "first-fruits" of students for an awakening that spanned a period of ten to twenty years and covered a huge geographical area of the United States. It was also the catalyst for new home and foreign mission work that required more trained spiritual leaders. The need for more schools and more students was still very great. The Lord was working on that problem as well. Many of these "first-fruits" students of the early college revivals, such as Lyman Beecher, Ashabel Green, Edward Griffin, Heman Humphrey, William Sprague and many others, went on to become the new presidents of some of the leading New England schools, such as Princeton, Brown, Williams, and Rutgers. Some of these men became the founders of many new evangelical schools and seminaries in both the southern and western territories of the United States.

William Speer, another of the men who experienced the Second Great Awakening, made the following observation: *The cause of Ministerial Education is one of the first to feel the influences of a genuine outpouring of the Holy Spirit; and these influences, it soon sends streaming in an energized generation of ministers, through every branch and fiber of the Church's outward life.*[97]

Reflect upon these thoughts and pray.

When you talk to college age young people today, how many are going to school for fulltime Christian ministry? Do you think today's Christian parents encourage or support their children who believe God is calling them into ministry? How does your church support or celebrate a young person's call into ministry? How would college revivals transform every aspect of our culture?

Lord, we are jealous of how you brought revival upon college campuses during the Second Great Awakening. We ask for the same outpouring of your Spirit to fall, first upon students who consider themselves Christians, and then upon entire student bodies. Place godly men and women in positions of authority on our college campuses. Amen.

(Daily reading: Ezra 8:1-12)

Day 38

The Haystack Gang

When we left young Samuel Mills on Day 30, he had left the farm and had enrolled at Williams College in Massachusetts. He went with his parents' blessing, having shared with them his heart's concern over the "miseries of perishing millions."[98] From that day on, Samuel Mills, Jr., set his mind upon preparing for fulltime ministry, with an eye toward foreign missions.

In 1805, Williams College was just beginning to experience the awakening. Students assembled together in conferences to seek prayer and counsel from each other, as they experienced the Spirit's conviction in their lives. Samuel Mills proved himself to be a true student leader during the awakening at Williams. While his scholarly abilities were respectable, he stood out among his peers as a shining light of spiritual devotion and moral integrity. He was respected by all the students, including the infidels on campus. Here was a young man whose walk with the Lord was so evident that many felt the reproach of his example and were led to Christ.

As Samuel Mills continued his studies, the Lord was preparing him to be a leader among his peers in what became the dawn of American foreign missions. Mills eventually gathered some of his closest friends around him to share his heart's desire. They found a remote spot near the banks of the Hoosic River, beside a haystack, and here Mills shared his heart with his friends. To his surprise, the Lord was also working in the hearts of his friends, giving them a similar burden for the lost around the world. The area around that haystack became a spiritual retreat.

Every Saturday afternoon, it was here that Samuel Mills, James Richards, Gordon Hall, and Luther Rice prayed and fasted for the Lord to send missionaries to the lost and to renew their own burning desire to be sent out for this very purpose.

> *"I had always refused," says the Dr. Griffin "such applications; but from the love I bore to him, I agreed to criticize one sermon a week. After that exercise, he would commonly sit, and draw letters very moderately and cautiously out of his pocket, and read passages to me on some benevolent project. At length I perceived that studying divinity with me had been quite a secondary object; that his chief object was to get me engaged to execute his plans. As soon as I discovered that, I told him to bring out his letters and all his plans, without reserve."*
>
> *-Dr. Edward D. Griffin, New Hartford, Conn.*

In the spring of 1808, in a lower room on the college campus, the Haystack Gang organized into a missionary society. Here, Mills and many others soon gathered to organize plans for future missions around the world. This small society faced an upward battle for foreign missions. There was a greater interest and demand for settling pastors and church planters in the western territories where thousands of people were migrating on a yearly basis. Samuel Mills and friends, however, had a four-fold plan to shine the light upon foreign missions. First, they introduced the subject to various ministers and Christian leaders, outlining both the grand purposes of foreign missions and the ways to accomplish them. Secondly, they reprinted and circulated sermons from two highly esteemed men—Dr. Griffin (a missionary sermon presented before the national Presbyterian Synod) and Dr. Livingston (a missionary sermon preached before the New York Missionary Society). The students paid for the printing of these sermons from their own meager means. The third part of the plan was to target key denominational church leaders by volunteering in their respective churches during their school vacations. They so endeared themselves to these pastors and their church members that these leaders had no choice but to listen to these zealous students talk about their concern for the lost souls around the world. The final part of their plan was to encourage fellow students to answer God's call to be foreign missionaries.

Mills and gang networked with students from other colleges who had similar passions. One of these students happened to be a young man from Yale College, Asahel Nettleton (Day 33), who was introduced to Samuel Mills through a mutual friend, Simeon Woodruff. There was also an attempt to form missionary societies on other college campuses. One student left Williams and enrolled at Middlebury College for this very purpose. Samuel Mills, having graduated in 1809, went on to Yale for resident studies and established a missionary society in this pro-revival college.

At Yale College, he and his new friend Asahel Nettleton began a missionary society and entered into a solemn covenant *to avoid all entangling alliances, and to hold ourselves in readiness to go to the heathen, whenever God, in His providence, should prepare the way.*[99] Within a few months, Mills left Yale with plans to reunite with Nettleton the following year (1810) at the newly established Andover Seminary. This reunion never took place. Nettleton was forced to take a job at Yale for one year in order to pay off his schools debts. Mills, however, went to Andover and was introduced to another zealous young man ready to serve the Lord as a foreign missionary.

Adoniram and Samuel

When we left Adoniram Judson (Day 21), he had enrolled at Andover Seminary in 1808, and within four months, he had dedicated his life to fulltime Christian ministry. Soon after his dedication to ministry, Judson read a printed copy of a stirring missionary sermon by a British minister, Dr. Claudius Buchanan, who was the chaplain of the British East India Company. Adoniram Judson was so moved by the sermon that he vowed to be the first American foreign missionary. When Samuel Mills appeared on the scene in 1810, the two men began a friendship that culminated in a missionary synergism that launched American foreign missions.

Within a few months, Mills, Judson, and other Andover Seminary students formed the American Board of Commissioners for Foreign Missions, commonly known as the American Board. The goal of this board was to secure funds and call missionaries for foreign mission fields. By 1812, Judson and six other missionaries had become the first American foreign missionaries commissioned to work in India. Within a decade, similar foreign mission boards were established by the Baptist, Presbyterian, and Methodist denominations.

Eventually, Judson moved on to pioneer missionary work in Burma, eventually translating the entire Bible into Burmese. Samuel Mills, on the other hand, never became a foreign missionary. Like his friend Asahel Nettleton, the Lord had other plans for him.

Reflect upon these thoughts and pray.

What impressed you the most about the missionary zeal of Samuel Mills and his friends? What do you think fueled their zeal to reach the lost?

Lord, we long to see that same missionary zeal that was evident in the Great Awakenings in our churches today. We pray that every people group will be reached in this generation. Awaken your Church and empower it to finish this Great Commission. For Your name's honor and glory, we pray. Amen.

(Daily reading: Revelation 7:9-17)

Day 39

The Year of the Lord's Favor

Isaiah 61 must have been a comforting message to the exiles in Babylon. They were prisoners in a foreign land, and engraved in their collective memories were the ashes of their former home—Jerusalem. Instead of wearing crowns as God's people, they were wearing ashes on their heads, and instead of clothes of celebration, they were wearing clothes of despair, shame and disgrace. However, a new day was about to dawn. Just as in the Year of Jubilee, the Israelites would once again see the Lord's favor. There would come a time when they would be released and free to rebuild the ancient ruins and "renew the ruined cities." The Spirit was upon Isaiah to preach this good news to the Jews over 200 years before it happened. Little did Isaiah know how these words would ultimately be fulfilled!

In Luke 4, Jesus preached a sermon to his hometown synagogue. He used Isaiah 61 as his text. His application of the passage was quite simple and yet earthshaking, *Today this scripture is fulfilled in your hearing* (4:21). The hometown folks missed the significance of Jesus' words. Their glowing pride in their hometown boy turned to anger as Jesus condemned their hard-heartedness. Little did they know how these words preached in their little village would ultimately be fulfilled!

The faithful few who were praying for the Year of the Lord's Favor in the eighteenth century, longed to see prisoners set free from the spiritual grip of deism, atheism, Unitarianism, Universalism, and hedonism. These faithful few looked upon their country and culture with tearful eyes of mourning that such a blessed nation had so quickly turned its back upon the Lord who had given her independence from British rule. They felt a measure of disgrace and shame that this nation was not what John Winthrop and the early settlers of America desired and prayed for America to be—"a city upon a hill." John Winthrop's sermon, *Christian Charity*, had been preached on the dawn of a great voyage, which had brought them to the shores of America to establish a plantation in Massachusetts. In Winthrop's sermon, he reminded these New England pioneers that if the Lord had brought them safely to the shores of America, they should view this as a mandate to be and live as God's servants in this new land. For Winthrop, this meant that they were to follow the words of the Prophet Micah, *"To act justly and to love mercy and to walk humbly with your God* (Micah 6:8). John Winthrop interpreted Micah's words and gave the faithful followers this commission: *to delight in each other, make other's conditions our own; rejoice together, mourn together, labor and suffer together—always having before our eyes our commission and community in the work, our community as members of the same body.*[100]

America was far from this goal in the late eighteenth century. But as the faithful remnant prayed, and the eighteenth-century Elijahs worked to rebuild the altars of the Lord, the Year of the Lord's Favor was about to dawn. Little did they know, as they prayed fervently, how the Lord was about to fulfill the words of Isaiah 61, even in their day.

> *During the time that the awakening continued, sports and pastimes, and ceremonious visits were generally discontinued; and the ball-room was so far unoccupied, that the musician found that his craft was in danger, and that his hopes of gain were gone. And in those days, the Word of the Lord, both read and preached were precious.*
>
> *-Rev. SImon Waterman 1799 Plymouth, Conn.*

As the Spirit awakened the Church, and thousands of people became liberated from the bondage of sin and guilt, seeking Christ only and His redemption, ancient ruins were restored and cities were renewed and became beacons of light. They became *a planting of the Lord for the display of his splendor* (Isa. 61:3). In their hearts, they desired to be "priests" and "ministers" of their God (vs. 6).

In these final two days of our journey, we will chronicle this change in order to encourage us to keep praying for a similar awakening. We begin with the moral and spiritual change that took place in lives, families, and entire communities.

Thomas Paine, Why Have You Come Back!

We've already pointed out how the day-to-day conversations in many New England towns had changed. People were talking about spiritual things at church, at work, in their neighborhoods, and even at weddings, according to Rev. Jeremiah Hallock of Canton, Connecticut.[101] There was something else happening in both New England and throughout the United States—a change of interests.

Awakened hearts were more concerned about doing God's will in their own lives and furthering His Kingdom in their cities and culture. Rev. David Rice said in a sermon preached at the opening of the Presbyterian Synod of Kentucky: *Yea, some neighborhoods, noted for their vicious and profligate manners, are now as much noted for their piety and good order. Drunkards, profane swearers, liars, quarrelsome people, etc. are remarkably reformed. The songs of the drunkard are exchanged for the songs of Zion; fervent prayer succeeds in the room of the profane oaths and curses; the lying tongue has learned to speak truth in the fear of God, and the contentious firebrand is converted into a lover of peace.*[102]

The awakening created a more serious and sober perspective in every aspect of life. Dance halls and frivolous social gatherings became unpopular. Awakened Christians, as Rev. Samuel Shepherd noticed, *have very uniformly appeared to be humble, and to walk softly before their Maker.* This should not be understood, however, to mean that life became rigid or joyless. Rev. Shepherd also prayed this prayer: *May a holy God, in infinite mercy, continue to make manifest the glory of his power, and the glory of his grace, in building up Zion; for in no other way can we rationally hope to see happy individuals—happy families—happy neighborhoods—happy societies—happy towns—happy states—happy kingdoms—and a happy world.*[103]

College campuses, once the hotbeds of French philosophers and gambling, experienced moral changes. In schools like Yale, new student-led societies soon replaced infidel clubs and anti-Christian groups. Revival historian J. Edwin Orr wrote that at Yale a "Student Moral Society" had formed, which discouraged profanity, immorality and intemperance. This society soon comprised close to half of the student body. He also cited Harvard, which had its own society called, "The Saturday Evening Religious Society," which was formed to combat French infidelity.[104]

From East to West, the tide of infidelity was turning. In New York State, the Rev. James Hotchkin wrote:

> The tide of infidelity, which was setting in with so strong a current, was rolled back and Western New York was delivered from the moral desolation which threatened it. The general prosperity the religious order, the benevolent and literary institutions which constitute the glory and happiness of this section of country, it cannot be doubted, are in no inconsiderable degree attributable to the change produced in the current public sentiment, as the consequences of this extended revival of religion. The year 1798 is an era which should long be remembered in Western New York, as giving a character to this part of the state which laid a foundation for its large prosperity and improvement in all things useful.[105]

Perhaps the most evident place where the awakening had transformed the moral and civil landscape was in Kentucky. If you remember Day 2, we noted that there were places in Ohio and Kentucky that were becoming hideouts for fugitives. There was little law and order in these places, with gangs of both foreign and domestic thugs abusing settlers and attacking Indians. However, huge changes had taken place as a result of the awakening, according to Dr. George Baxter, who wrote the following to a friend about his visit to Kentucky:

> The power with which this revival has spread, and its influence in moralizing the people, are difficult for you to conceive and more so for me to describe. . . I was informed by settlers on the road to Kentucky that the character of Kentucky travelers was entirely changed, and that they were now as remarkable for sobriety as they had formerly been for dissoluteness and immorality. And indeed, I found Kentucky, to appearances, the most moral place I had ever seen. A profane expression was hardly ever heard. A religious awe seemed to pervade the country.[106]

The moral and spiritual landscape had so drastically changed after the awakening, that when President Thomas Jefferson invited his old friend Thomas Paine to return to the United States from France in 1802, he realized that he had made a terrible political mistake. Jefferson had sent the naval sloop Maryland to retrieve Paine as an honored guest of the United States. As the naval sloop headed toward Baltimore, many newspapers attacked Paine for his anti-Christian militancy, and because he had previously attacked the character of George Washington. The outpouring of public opinion against Paine's return was so great that Jefferson regretted his connection with Paine's return. The New York Evening Post was so anti-Paine that they had vilified him publically in their December 8, 1802, edition:

To Tom Paine
Detested reptile! Wherefore has thou come
To add new evils to our groaning land?
To some wild desert let thy carcass roam.

Where naught can wither by thy blasting hand.
In the dark hour that brought thee to our shore,
The shade of Washington did awful scowl-
Hence, gloomy monster! Curse mankind no more
Thy person filthy as thy soul is foul.[107]

Reflect upon these thoughts and pray.

Imagine what our culture would be like today, if we experienced a similar awakening. Would all of our sports and entertainment be suspended, or would they be given a different priority and purpose in a time of awakening?

Lord, our hearts long to live in a society where spiritual things are the hot topics of the day, and where we and our families can live without fear of being abused. Pour out your Spirit with such transforming power that everyone may see and know "your planting" for the display of your splendor. Amen.

(Daily reading: Isaiah 61:1-7)

Day 40

Sun of Righteousness

Having grown up on a farm, I can appreciate the agrarian metaphors and examples given in the Bible. One of these farming metaphors comes out of Malachi 4:2, *And you will go out and leap like calves released from the stall.* I can still remember letting young calves out of the stalls in the spring of the year. These wintertime calves were put into small pens inside warm barns after they were born. Here they received milk until they were weaned off and fed "calf-crunch" (yes, there is such a thing). As the winter snows melted off, and the grass started to grow in the pasture, we pushed and pulled these calves out the door so their wobbling feet and hooves could grow accustomed to walking, and they could leave their small pens behind.

Eventually, as the calves smelled the fresh air of the outdoors and their eyes grew accustomed to the sunlight, they would raise their heads and kick their hind legs outward, leaping forward with the joy of freedom. What a powerful word picture to describe the feelings of victory and joy given to God's faithful people in every age! Whenever you doubt the promises of God and wonder if it pays to keep praying fervently and living faithfully, Malachi 4:2 reminds you that spring is coming!

Those who revere God's name receive a promise of healing here in Malachi. The sun of righteousness will rise, and when it does, there will be healing in its wings. The Jews had a saying about the rising of the sun—As the sun riseth, infirmities decrease. Things usually look better in the morning. Even Jeremiah looked forward to the morning sun, because he believed there would be new mercies from a faithful God (Lam. 3:22-23).

Now add Psalm 139:9-10 to the mix: *If I rise on the wings of the dawn, if I settle on the far side of the sea, even there your hand will guide me, your right hand will hold me fast.* David reminds us that we can't outrun the Lord. As the sun rises and its light quickly crosses the waters, and as the wings of a bird quickly glide over the face of the waters, so too comes the presence of the Lord.

Jesus is the ultimate fulfillment of all healing. As the Light of the World, and as the very embodiment of righteousness, Jesus brought both physical and spiritual healing each day as He walked on earth. As the morning sun rose over an empty tomb, He trampled down His enemies—death and the devil. The result of his victory brings Christians healing and the freedom to kick up their heels and trample down His enemies. Didn't Paul even encourage the Christians in Rome with this promise, *The God of peace will soon crush Satan under your feet* (Rom. 16:20)?

The Lord brought healing to many Christians and churches in the late eighteenth and early nineteenth centuries, both here in the United States and across the oceans. As the rays of God's grace quickly spread across the states and territories of the United States, the spiritual healing caused the Church to "kick-up its heels" and leap out of its dark spiritual captivity, filled with joy and the desire to free others.

In Day 38, we read about the Haystack Gang who longed to go out and be the first foreign missionaries from America. However, there were many others who desired to kick up their heels and serve the Lord in other ways and in other places.

Samuel Mills Jr., not only had a desire to bring the gospel message overseas, but he also felt called by the Lord to explore the western territories of the United States, with the goal of preaching the gospel to the destitute and promoting the establishment of Bible societies and other religious and charitable institutions. He made two trips, the first in 1812-13, and the second trip in 1814-15. What Samuel Mills found was a shortage of Bibles and other Christian resource materials. Mills believed that half a million Bibles were needed to meet the demand. This need prompted the establishment of the American Bible Society in 1816. Within a short period of time, Samuel Mills and fellow Andover classmate Daniel Smith brought westward a cargo of 5,000 French New Testaments, 600 English Bibles, and 13,000 tracts, which were given out to people living along the Ohio, Missouri and Mississippi Rivers.[108] In the next four years, the American Bible society distributed nearly 100,000 Bibles.

Mills logged some 3,000 miles on his first journey with Rev. John Schermerhorn, covering nearly every state and territory of the United States. With great zeal, he began to correspond with Bible and missionary societies to urge them to send Bibles and men out into these areas to plant churches. After his second trip with Daniel Smith, Mills once again sent an urgent plea for help: *The whole country, from Lake Erie to the Gulf of Mexico is as the valley of the shadow of death. Darkness rests upon it . . . This vast country contains more than a million inhabitants. Their number is every year increased by a mighty flood of emigration . . . Yet there are at present only a little more than one hundred ministers in it. Were these ministers equally distributed throughout the country, there would be only one to every ten thousand people.*[109]

Samuel Mills' plea for more pastors and Bibles was made known through the proliferation of Christian magazines, many reporting on the progress of the awakening and the advancement of God's Kingdom around the world. These monthly religious magazines, such as *The New York Missionary Magazine, The Connecticut Missionary Magazine, The Christian Remembrancer, The Western Missionary Magazine, The Baptist Watchman, Zion's Herald (Methodist),* and *The Morning Star* (Free will Baptist) were just a few of the sixty-three new magazines started in the United States from 1801-1810. These magazines not only reported what was happening overseas, raising much needed financial and prayer support, but they also acted as watchmen, reporting on the progress of the awakening in the United States. There were still churches in America who had not experienced revival. Documenting current revivals and how God was moving in various congregations stirred the hearts of many other pastors and church members to keep praying for God to move in their congregations. Some of these pastors found a powerful ally in the ministry of Asahel Nettleton.

Both Samuel Mills and Asahel Nettleton desired to be foreign missionaries, but the Lord desired the two men to work at home. The Lord used Nettleton as an evangelist in churches throughout New England and New York. He was acutely sensitive and obedient to the Spirit's leading concerning with which churches he should get involved as a traveling evangelist. He never began a work in a church unless he first had the support of the pastor. His sermons were anointed with power from above, reminiscent of George Whitfield in the First Great Awakening. Asahel Nettleton's ministry continued until he contracted typhus in 1822. Nettleton eventually returned to ministry two years later, but he never fully recovered his strength, and by the year 1826, the Second Great Awakening gave way to a new era that is often referred to as the age of "Revivalism." The Spirit moved with such power within these twenty years that while the general population of the United States tripled in size, the population of the Protestant Church increased five times over.[110]

Perhaps one of the greatest legacies of the Second Great Awakening was a budding sensitivity toward the plight of slaves in this country. The awakening in England changed the national perspective of slavery and, eventually, the practice itself, through the efforts of men like William Wilberforce and John Newton.

After Samuel Mills Jr., returned from his exploration of the South, his heart was stirred by the poor conditions of what he estimated were one and a half million slaves. He had also discovered that many slave owners in the South were ready to emancipate their slaves, if they could offer them a good future. Mills had suggested giving the emancipated slaves western territories in Indiana or Illinois. However, this proposal was rejected, because of the high rate of migration that was already taking place in these areas. Finally, an old solution was resurrected. Dr. Samuel Hopkins, a pastor from Rhode Island, had suggested that the slaves receive some form of restitution for the evil they had endured, and that some should even be educated and sent back to Africa as teachers and preachers of the gospel.

Mills, along with fifty others, signed a constitution called, The *American Society of Colonizing the Free People of Color in the United States.* Mills volunteered to go with a group to Africa to explore the Western Coast to look for the perfect place to begin such a colony. They found what they considered to be an ideal location. Although the Society did not actually begin the new colony until 1822, Mills left the coast of Africa believing that he had found a solution to eradicate America's involvement with slavery.

Sadly, Samuel Mills Jr., never made it home after he finished his mission. He developed a fever and a racking cough after being out two weeks at sea. On June 15, 1818, Samuel Mills Jr., died of tuberculosis. This young man's conversion and life have given us a glimpse of the true nature of great awakenings and why God sends them. His humble and yet dogged desire to make Jerusalem the praise of all the nations of the world is why God sent His Spirit to awaken the churches in the late eighteenth century. The generation of young people like Samuel Mills Jr., Asahel Nettleton, and Adoniram Judson were growing up in a culture that was quickly becoming post-Christian, just as our culture today has become. The Lord could have allowed this nation to continue down this path, but because of His great mercy and His desire to reach the nations of the world, He moved the hearts of many teary-eyed mothers and fathers, tired pastors, and troubled leaders to pray fervently for His Spirit to awaken the Church of their day.

Missiologists estimate that there are still 6,900 people groups left in the world that need to hear the gospel message. Of that number, 418 people groups are considered beyond the reach of the gospel at this time.[111] Does the Lord have a plan to use this very tech-savvy generation to reach the last of these groups in our lifetime? It seems like a pipedream when you consider the present spiritual state of our youth. How could a generation of young people, living in a post-Christian, sex-driven, relativistic, and self-absorbed culture ever become transformed and zealous for the glory of God to be revealed in their own country, let alone to the ends of the earth? *I'll answer that question with a question: Is not the God who transformed an earlier and equally post-Christian generation still God?*

We need the faith and firm conviction of Timothy Dwight and many others who not only prayed fervently, but also kept preaching and teaching the truth of God's word as they rebuilt the altars for God's fire to refine and to re-fire His Church.

> I love Thy kingdom Lord! The house of Thine Abode
> The Church our blest redeemer saved with His own precious blood.
>
> I love Thy Church, O God! Her walls before Thee stand
> Dear as the apple of Thine eye and graven on Thy hand.
>
> For her my tears shall fall, for her my prayers ascend
> To her my cares and toils be giv'n till toils and cares shall end.
>
> -Timothy Dwight, 1797

Reflect upon these thoughts and pray.

Do you believe that our God is able to transform this generation and culture so that our present day vices and injustices, like abortion, pornography, sexual abuse, and racism could be things of the past? What would our country look like and what would life be like in the United States, if these sins were made things of the past? If we believe that God is still God, and He is able to do this, why doesn't the Church fervently pray and ask Him to bring it about?

Lord, we long to see this present generation transformed and to see us zealous for your glory to be revealed, both in our culture and around the world. Awaken Your Church and bring healing, so that we may leap with joy into a world that has received healing transformation through Your Son's righteousness. Amen.

(Daily reading: Malachi 4)

Day 41

The Forty-first Day

(I Samuel 17:1-50)

David was told to bring an ephah of roasted grain and ten loaves of bread to his brother as well as ten cheeses to the commanding officer. All were "fighting" in King Saul's army against the Philistines. This was an unusual battle for the Israelites, because the Philistines had brought forward their prize fighter, a nine-foot-tall fighting machine named Goliath. The man must have been strong and muscular, because we are told that the point of his spear weighed close to fifteen pounds. That would be the same weight as three good sized bricks.

The challenge Goliath presented to the Israelites was a one-on-one, winner-take-all battle between himself and someone of the Israelites' choosing. They would fight to the finish, with the losing side becoming the captives of the winning side. From the Philistines' perspective, the offer seemed humane. The Philistines had all the weapons, whereas Israel had only two swords (I Samuel 13:22). The Philistines also had the giant fighting machine Goliath, who could have taken on a hundred men by himself. If the two sides had actually fought, Israel would have been annihilated. Regardless of the outcome, the Philistines would have claimed victory and triumphantly boasted that their gods were greater than the God of Israel.

For forty days and nights Goliath came forward, taunting and challenging Israel to find a man brave enough to take him on in battle. Ironically, Israel had an equally large man who could have given Goliath a competitive battle. We are told in I Samuel 10:23, that Saul stood a head taller than any of the others in Israel. However, Saul was terrified of the man. The only thing he was willing to sacrifice was a financial and matrimonial (the marriage of his daughter) reward to any man who would dare fight Goliath.

What a pathetic sight this must have been in the eyes of God. Not one man was willing to step forward and do something for the honor and glory of God's name, and for the future of the Israelite nation! All the Israelites did for forty days was talk about the problem and cower every time their huge nine-foot problem stepped forward.

However, on the forty-first day, a young shepherd boy came to the battle site with some bread and cheese. He became angry, and he asked questions: *Who is this uncircumcised Philistine that he should defy the armies of the living God?* (1 Sam. 17:26b). The time for talking about the problem had to stop. It was time for action! David stepped forward to meet the giant with a two-fold assurance and a five-stone slingshot. His assurance came from the fact that the Lord had delivered him from both a lion and a bear in the past, and he was fighting the Lord's battle. While the nine-foot-tall giant was standing in front of David, with eyes of faith David could see that God was taller and stronger than Goliath (Ps. 24:7-10), so he knew that his victory was assured.

In verse 46 of 1 Sam. 17, David gives the ultimate reason for his stepping forward to take on the giant: Today . . . *the whole world will know that there is a God in Israel. All those gathered here* (particularly Saul and the army of Israel) *will know that it is not by sword or spear that the Lord saves* (because Israel had neither one); *for the battle is the Lord's, and he will give all of you into our hands.* (My words in the brackets). The Lord was able to remove a nine-foot problem with just a simple slingshot, one stone, and one faith-filled young shepherd boy.

Our Forty-first Day

In the past forty days, you have read about what God did to awaken His Church here in the United States in one of the most degenerative times in our nation's history. A faithful remnant subdued a lion, a bear, and a huge Paine in the neck, and the Lord brought deliverance. You have also been challenged to action as we briefly stared down our Goliath-size issues of the day.

There are, and have been, many 40-day books and programs offered to churches and small groups. I am sure they have all added significant insights to the greater Christian community. Unfortunately, on the forty-first day, the Christian community moves on to the next 40-day program or study, with more talk and more commiserating together about daily issues and Goliath-size challenges. That is why this devotional booklet has a forty-first day. It is time for action!

All through this devotional, I have encouraged you to pray fervently for the next Great Awakening. Now is the time to step forward and commit yourself before the Lord to do at least one of the following things until the Lord brings about the next Great Awakening.

1. **Attend the weekly prayer group in your church**—pray for your pastor(s) to be a faithful servant, rebuilding the altars of the Lord with God's Word; pray for a spiritual awakening among the members of your church, especially the younger generation; and pray for every ministry, teacher, and leader to be protected against discouragement and all of the temptations that the enemy throws against them.

2. **If there isn't a weekly prayer group in your church—begin one with others** who share your burden, and who will fervently pray with you. Ask the Lord to lead people to you if you are hesitant to ask. Be sure to invite your pastor(s).

3. **Begin a monthly prayer group in your church for anyone who has a burden for prodigals**—their own children and grandchildren—or who has a burden for the generation that has walked away from the Church.

4. **Take part in or establish a pastor's monthly prayer time** as a pastor or as a full-time laborer of the kingdom. Pray for each other, but also pray fervently for the Lord to move among your congregations, cities, and neighborhoods.

5. **Approach neighboring churches and fellow Christians to set aside one day a quarter for a concert of prayer.** This day should include church-wide prayer and fasting and an evening or noontime gathering of Christians from the various neighborhood churches.

6. **Begin to sow the seed of God's word on a regular basis in your neighborhood and/or city.** If you give out physical bread, make sure you also give out the Bread of Life. As you sow the seed, begin praying for every household around your church and in your own neighborhood.

Endnotes

Textbox Quotes

Page 56- Bennet Tyler, New England Revival, (Boston: Massachusetts Sabbath School Society 1846) pg.102

Page 73- Samuel Orcutt, The History of Torrington, (Albany: J.Munsell 1878) pg. 539

Page111- Tyler, pg.182

Page 115- Ibid. pg.186

Page 138- William Speer, The Great Revival of 1800 (Philadelphia: Presbyterian Board of Publication 1872)

Page 141- Tyler, pg.66

Page 144- Frank Grenville Beardsley, A History of American Revival (New York: American Tract Society 1912) pg.92

Page 157- Tyler, pg.246

Page 161- Ibid, pg.225

Page 162- Speer, pg. 65

Page 170- Ibid, pg. 85

Page 174- Tyler, pg.

General Endnotes

[1]Joel Parker in a 1794 sermon entitled "Revival Sermon"

[2]As quoted in David McCullough's book, John Adams (New York: Simon and Schuster 2001) pg.529. Sadly, Charles Adams died on November 30, 1800, with what was likely cirrhosis.

[3]Daniel Dorchester, The Problems of Religious Progress (New York: Philips and Hunt 1881) pgs. 182-183

[4] Peter Cartwight, Autobiography of Peter Cartwright (New York: Abingdon Press 1956) pg.30

[5]It was reported that anti-Christian Frenchmen had financed this project with over 3 million francs to print and distribute the writings of Paine and others to the youth of America. (A.B. Strikland The Great American Revival, pgs.32-33)

[6]Lyman Beecher writes in his biography that he would read Thomas Paine in the barn lest he upset his uncle and aunt. (Autobiography I, 43)

[7]Elihu Palmer, Principles of Nature (London: Sidwell and Kneas 1823) p. 112

[8]James D. Richardson, A Compilation of the Messages and Papers of the Presidents 1789-1904 (New York: Bureau of Natl. Literature and Art, 1904) I:285

[9]Abner Cunningham, Practical Infidelity Portrayed (New York: Daniel Cooledge 1836) pgs42-46

[10]Erwin Lutzer and John DeVries, Satan's "Evangelistic" Strategy For This New Age (Wheaton: Victor Books 1989)

[11]Ibid. pg.93

[12]Timothy Dwight, p.376

[13]Leverette Wilson Spring, A History of Williams College (Boston: Houghton-Mifflin Company 1917) pg.60

[14]Ibid, pg. 60

[15] Timothy Woodbridge, An Autobiography of a Blind Minister (Boston: John P. Jewett and Company 1856) pg. 44

[16]F. Rudolph, The American College and University (Athens Georgia: University of Georgia Press 1990) p. 38

[17]Spring, pg. 62

[18]Rudolph, pg. 39

[19]Thomas Jefferson Wertenbaker, Princeton (Princeton: Princeton University Press, 1946) pg. 135

[20]William B. Sprague, Lectures on Revivals of Religion (Glasgow: William Collins 1832) pg.410

[21]Samuel Eliot Morrison, Three Centuries of Harvard (Cambridge: Harvard University Press, 1964) pg. 185

[22]Rudolph, pg.39

[23]Lyman Beecher, The Autobiography of Lyman Beecher (London: Sampson, Low, Son, and Marsten 1863) Vol. 1 pg.30

[24]Ibid, pg. 30

[25]George Fisher, The Life of Benjamin Silliman (New York: Scribner and Company, 1866) pg. 53

[26]Charles Cunningham, Timothy Dwight (New York: Macmillan Company 1942) pg. 302

[27]Ibid, pg.302

[28]William Speer, The Great Revival of 1800 (Philadelphia: Presbyterian Board of Publication 1872) pg.17

[29]Keith Hardman, The Spiritual Awakeners (Chicago: Moody Press 1983) pg. 116

[30]Rudolph, pg. 41

[31]Edward Judson The Life of Adoniram Judson (Philadelphia: American Baptist Publication society 1883) pg. 2

[32]Ibid. pg.2

[33]Ibid. pg.7

[34]Ibid. pg.11

[35]David Kinnamon, You Lost Me (Grand Rapids: Baker Books 2011) p.22

[36]Ibid, pg. 52

[37]Ibid, pg. 52

[38]John Duffy, Epidemics in Colonial America (Baton Rouge: Louisiana State University Press 1953) first four chapters

[39]Speer, Pg. 11

[40] Brian Edwards, Revival (Durham: Evangelical Press 1990) p. 37

[41]Such was the case after 9/11. In a September 13th interview, just days after the terrorist attack, Jerry Falwell was interviewed by Pat Robertson on the 700 Club; here he made the point that God caused this to happen to our nation because "throwing God out successfully with the help of the federal court system, throwing God out of the public square, out of schools. The abortionists have got to bear some burden for this because God will not be mocked. . .I really believe that the pagans and the abortionists and the feminists and the gays and lesbians. . . the ACLU, the People for the American Way. . .I point the finger in their face and say you helped this happen."

[42]Erwin Lutzer, "Who Will Rescue the Rescuers?," Moody Monthly, April 1986, pp 28-31,

[43]J.A. Motyer, The Day of the Lion (Downers Grove: Inter Varsity Press 1974) pg. 185

[44]Vance Havner, Road to Revival (New York: Fleming H. Revell Company) pg. 16

[45]Quoted from the book, Powers of Darkness, by Clinton Arnold, pg. 23

[46] The History of Torrington ( ) p.528

[47]Ibid, 539

[48]Ibid, p.544

[49]Ibid, 537

[50]Ibid, p.547

[51]Colin Wells, The Devil and Dr. Dwight (Chapel Hill: North Carolina Press 2002) pg. 72

[52]There were three basic tenets to Chauncey's new theology: God's love and mercy are too great to permit or even to actively choose people to spend eternity in hell. (The Bennevolence of the Deity published in 1784) The fall of Adam and Eve brought about the imperfection of man, who are prone to those excesses of passions and emotions often resulting in sin. But God, in His mercy, has endowed every human being with the capacity to overcome the passions and emotions that lead to sin and poor judgments through the act of a rational will. (Five Dissertations on the Scripture Account of the Fall, published in 1785). Because human beings have minds and are able to reason, hell is not eternal. Hell is a temporary state in which the soul undergoes trials which will last as long as it takes to reform even the most unrepentant of sinners so that they see the "reasonableness" of God's truth and join the saints in heaven. (The Mystery Hid, published in 1782 and 1784)

[53]Timothy Dwight, Theology Vol. 1, pg. 51

[54]Cunningham, pg. 298

[55]Timothy's mother, Mary, was so offended by her father's dismissal from the Northampton church that she refused to enter the sanctuary and preferred to sit in the vestibule. She would also travel twelve miles to a neighboring church to take communion. She finally transferred her membership to this church in 1783. (Charles Cunningham, pg. 102 in his book entitled, Timothy Dwight)

[56]Timothy Dwight, Theology I, Memoir of the Life of President Dwight, pg.4

[57]Timothy wrote the poem, "Conquest of Canaan," as well as many patriotic songs during his time as a military chaplain in 1774, The song, "Columbia!," is perhaps the most familiar. Timothy also wrote a number of hymns, the most familiar one being, "I Love Thy Kingdom Lord."

[58]Dwight's spiritual renewal came soon after a period of convalescence at home in Northampton when he was close to death. In his attempt to learn and be able to read more each day, he avoided any physical exercise and for six months limited himself to twelve bites of food per meal. He eventually limited himself to only twelve bites of vegetables. The resulting diet brought on several attacks of colitis and when his father came to take him home before the summer break, many thought they would never see him again. The emaciated Dwight soon recovered from his near death experience and returned to Yale to begin his second year of teaching.

[59]Timothy's father was in Mississippi clearing ground in the area of Natchez. These titled areas were to be given to two of Timothy Dwight's brothers, but a sickness suddenly overcame Timothy's father, and he died. Sadly, the title of the land was misplaced, and the family lost their rights to the land.

[60]Dwight, pgs. 23-24

[61]Annabelle S. Wenzke, Timothy Dwight (Lewistown, NY: The Edwin Mellen Press, 1989) pg. 35

[62]Dwight understood with prophetic clarity how Chauncey's universalism would open up the floodgates of French philosophy to pour into the American churches. The author recommends Colin Wells' book, The Devil and Doctor Dwight, (2002 Chapel Hill) as an excellent study of Dwight's poem and its literary and theological context.

[63]Cunningham, pg.301

[64]Judson, pg.10

[65]Ibid, pg. 12

[66]Unitarianism in America developed as a reaction against historic church orthodoxy and Calvinism. William Ellery Channing best summarized their views at the time in an 1819 installation sermon for a new pastor in Baltimore. Simply put, Unitarians believe Jesus

is not God, but is inferior to God, and that he was sent by God to live as a moral example and a teacher. His death and resurrection merely proved a future life. "We further agree in rejecting as unscriptural and absurd the explanation given by the popular system (Historic Orthodox Christianity) of the manner in which Christ's death procures forgiveness for men. . . We ask for one text, in which we are told, that God took human nature that he might make an infinite satisfaction to his own justice. . ." pg. 102 Issues in American Christianity, by Keith Hardman (Grand Rapids: Baker 1993)

[67]J. Edwin Orr, The Eager Feet (Chicago: Moody Press, 1975) p.66

[68]W.H. Foote, Sketches of Virginia ( ) p.413

[69]Jonathan Edwards, An Humble Attempt to Promote Explicit Prayer" (Edinburgh: The Banner of Truth Trust, 1989) Vol. 2 pg.283

[70]Jonathan Edwards, Thoughts on Revival (Edinburgh: The Banner of Truth Trust 1989) Vol. I pg.426

[71]David Prior, The Message of Joel, Micah, and Habakkuk (Downers Grove: Intervarsity Press 1998) pg.76

[72]Gardiner Spring, The Memoirs of the Rev. Samuel J Mills (London: Francis Westley, 1820) pg. 5

[73]Ibid. pg. 9

[74]Speer, pg. 42

[75]Tyler, pg.28

[76]Tyler, pg.95 (Rev. Samuel Waterman from Plymouth Conn.)

[77]Ibid, pg. 66

[78]Speer, pg. 21

[79]Ibid, pg. 27

[80]Ibid, pg. 37

[81]Bennet Tyler, Memoirs of the Life and Character of Asahel Nettleton (Boston: Doctrinal Tract and Book Society 1844) pg. 64

[82]Ibid, pgs.96-97

[83]Ibid, pgs.195-196

[84]Ibid, pg. 37

[85]Ibid, pg.185

[86]Speer, pg. 66

[87]Tyler, pg.155

[88]Ibid., pg.62

[89]Speer, pg.47

[90]Tyler, pg.93

[91]Ibid, pg.85

[92]Tyler, pg.20

[93]Speer, pg. 58

[94]Cartwright, pg. 33

[95]Frank Grenville Beardsley, A History of American Revival (New York: American Tract Society 1912) pg. 89

[96]J. Edwin Orr, The Eager Feet (Chicago: Moody Press 1975) pg. 80

[97]Speer, pg.86

[98]The History of Torrington, pg. 551

[99]J.F. Thornbury, God sent Revival (Grand Rapids: Evangelical Press 1977) pg. 41

[100]Francis Bremer, John Winthrop (New York: Oxford University Press 2003) pg. 179

[101]Tyler, New England Revival, pg. 48

[102] Speer, pg.64

[103] Tyler, pg. 159

[104] J. Edwin Orr, The Eager Feet, pgs. 80-81

[105] James H. Hotchkins, History of Western New York (New York: 1848) pg. 42

[106] Speer, pg. 60

[107] Hardiman, The Spiritual Awakeners, pg. 114

[108] Benjamin Rice Lacy, Revivals in the Midst of Years (Hopewell: Presbyterian Evangelistic 1968) pg.83

[109] Hardiman, pg.159

[110] Ibid., pg. 169

[111] Statistics come from “Global Frontier Missions” and “Finishing the Task”

Reaching America County by County

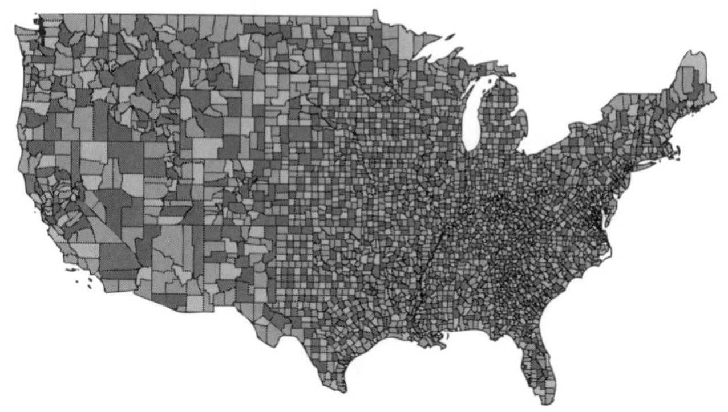

Let's begin to sow the seed of God's Word in every household across America!

Mail a copy of *Freedom From Fear* to everyone in your county. For more information contact us at reachingamerica@projectphilipministries.org.

Why Pray?

40 easy to read meditations about the joy of communicating to our Heavenly Father and trusting in Him.

(Available in both print and e-book formats)